A Winter Sabbatical

A Winter Sabbatical

Returning Home in Middle Age to Cornbread, the Northern Lights, and Wolves

Judythe Pearson Patberg

(Mostly) Minnesota Editions
2008

Copyright © 2008 by Judythe Pearson Patberg.

- Photo, front cover: Minnesota sunset
- Photo, back cover: The author and Hannah; graduation, 2007
- To order copies of the author's previous titles, *We Just Shoveled Two Feet of Partly Cloudy* and *From Peace Corps with Love*, please contact:

  (Mostly) Minnesota Editions
  2307 Gibley Park; Toledo, Ohio; 43617
  jpatber2@utnet.utoledo.edu

Library of Congress Control Number: 2008904707
ISBN: Hardcover   978-1-4363-4460-9
                    Softcover   978-1-4363-4459-3

To order additional copies of this book, contact:
Xlibris Corporation
1-888-795-4274
www.Xlibris.com
Orders@Xlibris.com
47772

This is my homeland,
The place I was born in—
No matter where I go,
It's in my soul.

My feet may wander,
A thousand places—
But my heart will take me back home
To my Donegal.

"Home to Donegal" from *Daniel O'Donnell Greatest Hits*

What if I don't have a chance to make new memories?
I'd better be fiercely tenacious in preserving those I have.

To Northern Minnesota: Past, Present and Future

To my sons who are young men now—
Will: a confident Californian with strong Minnesota ties,
married to lovely Jenny;
Zach: a fiercely independent newspaper reporter,
living on the East Coast; and
Jon: a passionate consumer of life experiences,
working in Bolivia.

And to Bill

Jon, Will, Bill, Zach, and Dad at the *Jakt Stuga*

Dear Daddy,

I really miss you a lot! We've been here for only a week now but I think of you every night and sometimes I even forget what you look like!!! I really can't wait until you come up here for Christmas. We are going to have the best time ever.

School's going great! My teacher's name is Mr. Klotz. He is really nice and he is even the principal! We have four recesses a day. A half an hour one in the morning, a 15-minute one at 10:00, one at lunch and one after school. Mr. Klotz teaches 5th and 6th grades at one time, just like Grandma (but she teaches first and second). Teachers don't seem to give you as much homework as they do at Central, but I think it's harder here. The grading system is strict.

The bus ride is an hour long so it's a long wait. I sit in the way back with Chris and we watch this kid named Looey chew tobacco and spit it behind the seats. On Friday I was trying to do the rest of my Social Studies homework on the bus and I got car sick and I threw up all over the place. It was really gross and I was embarrassed, but Looey thought it was funny. When I got to school I decided not to say I was sick and I was fine for the rest of the day.

At school we've been playing football but they're getting the ice rink ready so we'll be able to skate next week. Today I played with Tony and Zach. We were sledding on the hill and then we went on to the rink (there was a layer of ice on it and it was slippery). We were pushing each other on sleds and ramming into other kids on sleds!!! It was a lot of fun.

We're living at Grandpa and Grandma's now but I think we're going to move to Uncle Ed's house soon. All of the uncles and Grandpa have been working there. The pipes are frozen and the heater doesn't work. Zach and I are excited about roughing it there. But it's fun here too.

Dad, well I got to go. I love you a lot and I really miss you. How is the law business? I hear you got a new, bigger TV so you won't miss us so much.

Love your oldest son,
Willard

Introduction

The year was 1989. It had been 17 years since I returned from my Peace Corps experience in the Philippines. I had met and married my husband Bill and accepted an academic position at The University of Toledo where I was still on the faculty. Bill and I and our three sons had just moved into our new house with a big yard and a wonderful kid-friendly neighborhood in a bedroom community outside of the city. We had purchased our first computer two years ago—about the same time Bill quit smoking—and both events were changing the way we were doing things. I had been given Bill's grandmother's china, and I loved the way it looked on my new dining room table. My career was stable, having published enough to earn me full professorship with tenure, and I felt fulfilled. Bill was enjoying success as a lawyer, while managing to avoid the pitfall of workaholism in favor of spending time with our boys who were active in sports, music, and school-related projects. We had numerous friends, some very close to us. There were times when we wished that we lived closer to one of our families—either on the East Coast or in Minneapolis—but our Toledo friends had become our extended family with whom we celebrated birthdays and other important occasions. We were the quintessential middle-class suburban family.

I don't know when the idea of taking the boys to Minnesota for a few months came to me—probably when I was mulling over plans for a sabbatical. It was my 13th year at UT and time for my second sabbatical (definitely one of academia's strongest selling points—receiving a paycheck for taking time to rejuvenate every seven years). The problem was that this time I couldn't think of anything specific I wanted to do, except to take a break from teaching. Then it came to me: I would do a piece of research that examined the methods of teaching reading to children in small, rural communities and compare them with those used by teachers in large, suburban classrooms. As part of my data collection, I would observe classroom instruction in the small town where I grew up, including the first and second grades my mother taught. At the same time, I could offer my boys—ages four, eight, and ten—the experience of a small town, rural education along with time spent with their cousins and grandparents on the farm.

The idea took hold when Bill gave me his blessing. I don't think I've ever loved him more than when he told me I could leave and take his sons away from him for four months. I was touched by his generosity.

My application for a sabbatical almost wrote itself (which I took as a sign). Apparently, my department chair and the various committees that evaluate proposals decided that mine was meritorious in its potential benefits for the university, its students, and my professional career. It was approved without reservation.

So there we were—on the toll road heading North and West. The excitement we all felt at the prospect of a new adventure was mixed with some trepidation that things wouldn't work out, and the boys would miss their father too much. There was also some guilt lurking in the back of my mind, but I tried not to bring it to the forefront. I was determined to make this sabbatical work because it had turned into the most important undertaking in my life. Characteristically, once the idea was born, it didn't take much to convince myself that it was the right thing to do, and then it was full steam ahead—no doubts, reservations or questions about the validity, fairness or logic of the plan.

We were driving in blizzard conditions—snow coming down so hard and fast that we could barely see the road. The windshield wipers couldn't remove the snow quickly enough, so we had to stop and clean off the windows every once in a while. At one of those stops, the boys got out of the car to go to the bathroom on the side of the road. It was cold and I urged them to hurry up and get back in the car. We drove on for about an hour when Willie yelled, "Lucy's not in the car! She must have gotten out when we did!" Without thought or discussion, I whipped the car around, using a crossing for emergency vehicles only, and drove in silence. No one dared speak. Our eyes peeled to the road and our anxiety mounting by the minute, we were all thinking the same thing: How could we possibly find our little black and white dog on the Ohio Turnpike in a blizzard? Jonathan started whimpering.

"There she is, Mom, I think I see her!" yelled Zach. I almost swerved the van off the road in an attempt to identify the now mostly white form trudging through the thick snow on the side of the road—heading west to Chicago. She had crossed six lanes of traffic as if she knew that we would be coming back for her, and she had to be on the other side of the road in order for us to see her. Before I could come to a full stop, the boys opened the door and Lucy jumped in, shivering and wet. She had chunks of ice on her feet and nose, a sight that endeared her to us forever. She immediately curled up under the blanket on the seat between the boys, who took turns rubbing her down until she stopped shaking and, presumably, felt safe again. I marveled at our little dog's intelligence, tenacity, and courage.

In writing my account of the four months I lived on the farm where I grew up and had left twenty-five years ago, I used journals I kept during my sojourn, along with information I gathered from notes and every form of "hen-scratching" I had saved, including calendars and napkins. I am an unapologetic recorder of almost everything in my life—feelings and impressions as well as ideas and events. I'm also an incorrigible pack-rat; nothing gets thrown away. I offer this information about myself, so that any reader who wants to spend some time in my past can be assured that what is recorded in these pages are the real thoughts, people, and happenings of that period, and not ones I've made up. Of course, I've edited the content for spelling and grammatical correctness.

Judythe Pearson Patberg
April 24, 2008

One

December 14, 1989

Dear Bill—

. . . . Well, a decision has been made. We're moving in with Pam and Wayne. The situation at Uncle Ed's is too chancy, and we really need to get settled someplace. Wayne and Pam want us to live with them, and I must admit that life will be a lot easier because we can be self-sufficient in their basement and yet not have to worry about plumbing, electricity, etc. You should see the little bedroom Wayne built for me—complete with a desk. He also installed a bunk bed for the boys. I know we'll be happy here, and you will be relieved at not having to worry about us. I'm sad though, because I know that no one will ever live at "the Homeplace" again. We were the last takers.

I'd better get these letters out to the mailbox. Don't worry—the boys are fine. We all miss you and are eagerly anticipating your Christmas visit. Until then, take care.

Love,
Judy

It's January 3rd, and we've been in Northern Minnesota for a month already. I set out from Sylvania, Ohio on December 2nd

13

with my three sons and dog Lucy. I had four objectives in mind: to prove Thomas Wolfe wrong, i.e., one can go home again; to provide an opportunity for my boys to experience a little of the country life I knew while growing up; to rejuvenate myself; and to catch up on my academic reading, writing, and research. Now, four weeks later, it's time to examine these objectives to determine if any or all are in the process of being met.

Do I have a sense of "being home?" Yes and no. My surroundings are relatively unchanged and familiar, but I can't honestly say that I've been able to pick up where I left off twenty-five years ago. Too much has happened in my own life and in the lives of my family to fit in perfectly. My sisters look at things in such a way that I'm puzzled much of the time by their responses to people and events. They, in turn, probably think that my responses are strange. I often feel like an outsider when we're all together, even though they don't mean to exclude me. I can't be conspiratorial with them, not yet anyway. In some ways I feel closer to my sister-in-law than I do to my sisters. Maybe it's because I don't know Pam well enough to be intimidated so that I can be honest with her, not needing her approval as desperately as I need that of my sisters. Actually, I find everyone up here to be intimidating because they all seem to be so consistently sure of themselves. Bill thinks that I'm a self-confident person but I've never thought of myself that way, and I think that even less when I'm with my family. Maybe self-confidence is relative: I'm confident of who I am and what I believe unless I'm with my siblings who unintentionally make me feel unsure of everything.

My brother continues to be an enigma, and I don't feel as if I know him any better now than before I arrived. Being twelve years older than Wayne, I've never been able to spend enough time with him to really get to know him. I want his friendship badly. Perhaps the age and distance barriers we've lived with so long will make a close friendship difficult, or maybe, just maybe, family genes and ties are strong enough to make it happen. Time will tell, I suspect.

Dad is an interesting person whose company I enjoy. I want to please him, but we have a complicated relationship. Sometimes we have a complete communications breakdown that leaves me feeling embarrassed, foolish, or just plain mad. Both of us are opinionated, stubborn, and strong-willed, so it's no wonder that we retreat to the no-speaking zone at times. But I'm confident that our love for each other will provide more smooth-sailing as time goes on. The imprints of my father, planted in my childhood, greatly affect me, even today.

I feel totally comfortable with Mom. She is an intelligent, kind, and giving person who works too hard, and I'm determined to make life a little easier for her while I'm here. The only worry I have is that I will hurt her feelings because she is so sensitive.

Both of my parents are accorded limitless love and respect by all of us. It's always been that way. In fact, when my sons show me love and respect, I feel they are echoes of my own childhood.

I've always felt good about being the oldest child, thinking that since I was born first, I must be first in my parents' hearts. Of course that's not true, but the possibility made me feel special growing up.

I haven't lived with these wonderful people for twenty-five years, so I don't know how I could have expected to fit in easily and naturally at the beginning. Time and distance have necessarily reduced my relationships with them to an informative exchange of letters and phone calls, along with summer vacations and an occasional trip together. I have felt homesick so often over the years, that to now interact with my family on a daily basis is something very new and wonderful. With the exception of Mom and Dad, I suspect that everyone most likely feels pretty tentative toward me also.

My hometown has changed considerably. Roseau is no longer the quaint little village where I grew up, inviting familiarity and security as it once did. It has expanded to the point where it is thoroughly modern with many of the amenities of a city, including a fast food restaurant (Hardy's). Except for family, neighbors, close friends of my parents, and a few of my high school friends who still live here, I know almost no one. I'm at the same time disturbed and relieved by this change, craving some familiarity but liking the anonymity.

Warroad, however, doesn't seem to have changed as much and retains the small-town atmosphere of my growing-up days. I'm glad about that, for I really don't want things up here to change at all.

Our plan was to live two miles away from my parents' farm at my Uncle Ed's house, the "Homeplace" where my Dad grew up, so the boys could experience the simplest life possible in this day and age. We had to abandon the idea after numerous failed attempts to overcome the kind of electrical and plumbing problems that could prove to be disastrous. My disappointment is great, and I can hardly bear to go over there for the loss that overwhelms me. All of them—Mom, Dad, my brother, sisters, and brothers-in-law—had worked so hard to make the house livable after years of neglect, and the result was a cozy place to call our home for a few months. The small fatalistic part of me says that it wasn't meant to be. But I must admit to indulging in a little "If only we had . . . . " thinking now and then.

So, after weeks of living out of suitcases and shuffling back and forth from Uncle Ed's to Mom and Dad's, we are pretty much settled in Pam and Wayne's basement, an alternative I'm definitely not unhappy about. The boys are a little disappointed but also happy that they will be living in the same house as their cousins. They had bragged to their friends in Sylvania that they were going to live like pioneers—no indoor plumbing or running water and I would be baking bread everyday. Instead we have all the comforts of home, surrounded by the people we came up here to get to know a little better. Life is good.

It's time to look at objective number two, the kids' experience. Evidence thus far suggests that this objective will be fully met. The boys are having a great time at the school where my mother teaches. We all get up at 6:00; Mom leaves for school at 6:15; the boys and Katie and Linsay meet Jenny, Chris and Tony at the bus stop at 7:00; and they all arrive at Malung School at 8:00. Even during the week when it was 40 below zero and they had to greet the bitterly cold morning in total blackness, there were no complaints.

At first Malung School was an adventure and now it's getting to be just plain school, I think. On the first day, Zach's enthusiastic comment was, "School is different and it's funner!" Willie was all smiles because he gained instant popularity. Katie said, "Auntie Judy, he made friends with everyone!" My assessment of the curriculum is that for Zach, third grade is easier and for Willie, sixth grade is harder than at Central School in Sylvania. Except for a weekly spelling test, Zach has no homework. Mrs. Hedlund, his teacher, told Mom that Zach is "a very nice boy." He's in the same grade as Linsay but plays primarily with Tony and his friends who are in the fourth grade. His papers look like those he brought home from his old school—mostly As. He made the C Squirt hockey team and is happy with that accomplishment, given the fact that his entire hockey experience consists of only one season in Sylvania. The players had to sign up for positions after practice yesterday and Zach said he was going to tell the coach he wanted to play defense because "I would humiliate myself playing wing." When it came time to choose a position though, he said he preferred left wing—it's the soccer influence. Tony made the B team. I can hardly wait until they have a game.

Willie is studying European civilization—ancient Rome—in social studies and he likes it. He had his first open book test, which he thought was going to be a snap since Mr. Klotz allowed the students to use crib sheets. On the day of the test though, he came home from school feeling unsure of his performance. He said the test didn't include very many items he could answer based upon his crib sheet information. The next day his fears were confirmed: he got a C plus. "I must not have written down all the information on my card that Mr. Klotz thought was important, Mom, because I had answers for only three questions," he said. Tomorrow they have another test and he says he'll get an A. The grading system here is more rigorous than at their old school—straight percentages with 92% being a B, etc.

Will is playing basketball with a 6th, 7th, and 8th grade team combination. He's on the B team primarily because of his grade. I can't tell for certain how much he's enjoying it. He wants to go to practice but, when I probe, he says that the boys don't pass to him very much. However, in a letter he wrote to his grandparents, he said, "Basketball is going great. Even though I'm new here I get the ball a lot more than I used to so I guess I'm getting better." I'll get a more accurate picture when they play their first game; the truth probably lies somewhere in between the two perceptions.

Both boys say they have a lot of fun at recess. They mostly skate on the outdoor hockey rink and think that huddling around the barrel stove in the warming house when they get cold is awesome. When they're not skating, they're sledding on the hill and building forts in the woods—the very things I did when I was in grade school. In the same letter to his grandparents, Willie wrote, "School's going great. I'm getting good grades and making a lot of new friends." He added that he likes doing the different winter activities, such as skating (has a little trouble, never having done much of that), snocatting and hockey games. Will is a people pleaser, so it's hard to know sometimes if he says things that he really believes or those things he knows people want to hear. Zach, on the other hand, is an easy read. In his letter to his grandparents, he simply stated that he loves it here, and I believe him. Both of them have mentioned that they miss their old friends back in Sylvania and like to talk about what they might be doing at any given time. Their conversations go something like this:

"Hey, Willie, what do you think you'd be doing in Sylvania right now?"

"I don't know—school, homework, fooling around—you know, the same old things."

"Yeah, me too, here at least we're doing something different."

Will has release time from school for religious instruction at the Roseau Covenant Church once a week. He likes going, especially because of Pastor Joe Elick who thinks Willie is a great kid and an excellent Biblical scholar. Both compliments make me feel good. Then, on Wednesday nights, he and Zach go to church with Tony, Chris, Jenny, Katie, and Linsay for Adventure Club and Youth Group. They are always excited afterwards—eager to tell me what they did and how Tony got in trouble (with more than a little help from Zach, I suspect). I can't help but think that the Christian fellowship and fun is an important aspect of their experience here.

Then there is soon-to-be-five-year-old Jonathan who is having the time of his life. His days are filled with lots of busy activity centering on Roslyn and Grandpa. He and Rozie are best friends, but competition never fails to liven things up from time to time. Rozie has a slight competitive edge over Jon. She's aware of her developmental superiority and has a tendency to display a smug attitude that Jon finds infuriating. "I can't stand that smile Rozie always has on her face," he says, or "Rozie is so bossy." Occasionally, when Jon gets the best of her she pouts.

"To think he's going to be here a year," she lamented one day! Another time I was complimenting Rozie on how good she was for listening to me and, even though I didn't reprimand Jon, he knew that his behavior wasn't up to par. "Good, good, good," he sighed, "I get so tired of hearing how good Rozie is." Dad gets a big kick out of their competitive bickering.

Every day the two of them help Grandpa feed the cows, and sometimes he reads to them in his bed where they'll take a nap. They "play skirts" and do a lot of "homework" such as drawing and writing. In the evenings, Jon will run over to Mom and Dad's "to see what Grandma is doing." He's not afraid of walking the path in the woods from Wayne's house to Mom and Dad's, even in the dark. "It would take more than a walk in the dark to rile up that kid," Wayne mentioned one day, "he's a pretty easy-going little fellow."

The answer to the question of whether the boys are enjoying their experience is a "yes," I believe. They seem to thrive on their routine—go to school, have a snack, snocat, play with their cousins, and watch favorite television shows. Starting next week, though, they're going to start practicing the piano and reading again, and they'll probably complain because their playing time will be shortened. Really—I have to ask myself if it is necessary for them to pursue these things now. I can be so rigid at times!

As far as my third objective goes—rejuvenating myself—I feel certain that this will be accomplished during my sojourn. I've already lost a little weight so I'm feeling better about myself. I haven't been dieting but I haven't felt the need to overeat either so, hopefully, the pounds will disappear. Even though the days are busy, they aren't hectic, or even hurried, and I don't feel stressed out so that I yell at the kids, stuff myself, or get generally depressed. I wake up at 6:00, get the kids off to school, prepare for the day, wash dishes and clean up at "our place" (Pam and Wayne's), run over to Dad's to decide what

I'll make for dinner (that's the noon meal here on the farm) and read for an hour before I have to go back to Dad's to make dinner for him, Roz, and Jon. After cleaning up and getting the kids ready for Dad's stories and a nap, I have a couple of hours for reading and writing. I feel calm and serene—utterly content in my peaceful surroundings. I feel a kinship with this environment—the permanence of the farm; the absence of change; the security in knowing that I'll find the same people, the same animals, the same buildings whenever I return.

Sometimes I convince myself that I've chosen a course of action that seems narcissistic—leaving my husband, once again always wanting (and getting) more than I deserve. When I'm in this frame of mind, melancholia overtakes me. Not often though. I was born an optimist. I awaken each morning, filled with hope and anticipation. I thank God for the day, regardless of what is in store for me. I know that I have an annoying (to some people) tendency to view the world through rose-colored glasses. No matter how bad a day has been, there is always tomorrow, and tomorrow will be a better day. Things will fall into place and if I want something badly enough, it will happen—eventually. I'm always dreaming about possibility. I can't help it; that is the way I look at the world. Having this outlook on life, it may surprise people to know that I love cloudy days and inclement weather—wind and snowstorms—a lot more than sunshine. I actually get tired of summer every year. It's just too hot and bright, and the days seem never to end. Maybe I prefer blustery weather because it makes me pay attention, so that I'm not just passing through this world, but fighting to collect and savor the moments.

Two

It snowed a couple of inches last night and we awoke to a winter wonderland—a glistening, crystal-clear day. Except for that week of bitter cold in the middle of December, our winter has been unusually mild with temperatures in the teens or at least above zero. We're all hoping for more snow so we'll be able to do some distance snocatting soon. That wish alone makes me cognizant of how the winters up here have changed. I can't remember ever having to worry about enough snow to fill the snocat trails!

Willie and Zach have started practicing the piano again, and I realize how much I had missed that background "noise." One of the best decisions Bill and I made early on in our marriage (at least I think it was good!) was requiring our children to learn an instrument so that music would always be a part of their lives. There was no negotiation. Now, I love to watch them practice. Zach, baseball cap perched ubiquitously on his blond head bent over the piano and tongue out, pounds out Beethoven with the same intensity that he plays sports. Willie's playing is also like his soccer: calm, smooth, polished—each note precise and correct.

Zach missed the bus the other day so Gayle had to stop at Malung School on her way home from work and pick him up. Mom said he came into her classroom after school, worried that I would be angry with him for missing the bus. He told her he had had a very busy day and was feeling a little lonesome for Sylvania. When Mom suggested that he wished he were home he said, "No, I'm glad I'm here, Grandma. I like it but I'm just a little lonesome is all." I'm glad I didn't reprimand him when he got home. Instead, I suggested that missing the bus was no big deal.

At this point, I'm giving no thought as to how my fourth objective is going to be achieved. Anything academic is so far removed from my experience, I don't even think about doing scholarly reading and writing. I feel surprisingly little guilt. It was no accident that this objective was given fourth place on my list. While I do want to observe reading instruction in Mom's class (I think) and write a journal article on the instructional strategies and teaching methods she uses (I think), I'm not going to be disappointed if little gets done. As of this moment, if someone asked me how I was spending my sabbatical, I could say that I'm washing a lot of dishes, cooking, taking care of children, and savoring the serenity of farm life in the winter. For now, that's enough. I have a basic need to please, but feel so often in my life that I've disappointed, except for here where it's easy to please everyone.

A guy I've known for a long time asked me if this is a marriage sabbatical. "Have you run away?" he asked. If a marriage sabbatical is something you do when you have to get away from your husband then mine isn't one. The question did prompt me to think about my marriage though, and how it's always been a mixture of joy and anxiety—arguably more anxiety than joy lately. Maybe it will be helped by this sabbatical, after all. Maybe this sabbatical will, in some way, be able to infuse my marriage with the hope it needs. If that happens, the result will be a bonus!

It seems that as long as I immerse myself in my family, I don't have to think about myself: how I feel about relationships and what I really want to do with my life. I'm always waiting—for what, I'm not sure. My purpose in life right now, and for the next thirteen years, is to raise my sons so that they will someday do good things in the world. My purpose is very clear, but it hasn't always been so and will probably not be again when my sons leave home.

I'm pretty sure that our marriage can stand this period apart because my motivation is well-defined, and Bill knows my reasons for wanting to do this. Even though our marriage isn't rock-solid, it contains a basic level of trust that I don't think can be broken. Besides, Bill's nature is not to be jealous or suspicious. I can't get over the fact that he's giving me a most wonderful gift: letting me go without any guilt whatsoever.

I was a good girl growing up. I knew right from wrong. I obeyed my parents and did well in school. I had plans that were promised to all good girls: college, travel and career if desired; marriage and family, complete with the white picket fence. But life became complicated, and I have had to increasingly adjust my thoughts about happily ever after. I'm not sure, though, why I should expect my marriage to be perfect, to be even great most of the time, when I don't know many marriages that are.

If I had to do it all over again, I'd marry Bill in an instant. I know that because he's responsible for so much of the good in my life. And I do have my picket fence; it has to be painted more often than usual, probably, but painting it is worth the time and effort because the result is a shiny white.

Joyce came out one day with Jena who has finally warmed up to me. We cleaned Mom and Dad's whole house, Joyce doing the lion's share of work. She worked like a blitzkrieg, never stopping until the task was finished; it was rather amazing to watch! We were going to take my broken phone back to Karlstad but lost track of the time and abandoned the idea. We laughed a lot and generally fooled around. Joyce is a wonderful organizer and time manager, two qualities I wish I possessed.

Jena is darling—cute, smart and charming. She looks so much like Sharon, it's eerie!

A couple of days before Jon's birthday, we had a party for him at Mom and Dad's. Everyone, including Fred and Bev and Grandma Rosie, came over for chocolate M&M cake and ice cream. Jon had been anticipating the event all day and basked in all of the attention. He opened his presents with glee, all the while reminding people that this wasn't his "real" birthday. The highlight of the evening was a phone call from Bill. Jon had cried for him in the afternoon. When I reminded him that all the people at his party loved him, he wailed, "I know, but I want my Daddy too!" I overheard him say to Rozie later that she should be happy because she has her Daddy here and "you know, Rozie, I don't. It's going to be a long time until I see my Daddy and I miss him." Rozie corrected him, as she often does, by reminding him that he would see his Daddy in a few weeks when we go skiing at Boyne. When I confirmed that fact, Rozie must have given Jon the I-told-you-so look again because he protested, "Grandma, tell Rozie to quit smiling at me like she always does when she's right!" Those two make me laugh.

Everyone feels uneasy about this spring thaw in January (40 degrees one day!) because it violates the order of things. The weather is sunny and beautiful. It's amazing how rejuvenating a warm day can feel, especially after cold weather. The transition is so abrupt. I love winter, but can always appreciate a spring-like interlude.

We did some snocatting at Bemis Hill and it was a lot of fun. Zach rode with Dad, while Linsay rode with Wayne and Pam with me. Had we waited for another day there wouldn't have been sufficient snow—imagine! The country around Bemis Hill is some of the most beautiful in the world in the wintertime. The snow-clad evergreens and a small forest of birch trees surrounded us, and we felt like intruders in a silent world save for the steady low roar of the snocats. At one point, I heard Zach yell, "Awesome, just awesome!"

I'm always conscious of the beauty around me, and a snocat ride offers no exception. Every time we go for a ride, I can't help but be struck by the amazing providence of God in the great woods where we are so small. Sometimes melancholy overtakes me, I think because I know the day can be duplicated only so many times.

Willie and Chris were ice fishing with Uncle Rod and friends while we were snocatting. Will caught a two-pound walleye and Chris a four-pounder. Part of the fun for them was the overnight stay at Joyce and Rod's where they were allowed to watch TV until they fell asleep in front of the set.

Grandma Rosie is 86 years old and worthy of a queen's admiration. She is as feisty as ever. Right before Christmas, during that bitterly cold spell, she consented to spend the night with us only after we promised to get her back to town for her 9:30 hair appointment the next day. Well, the next morning none of the vehicles would start so she missed her appointment. Grandma was more than a little miffed. As she was leaving around noon, she announced that she wouldn't be spending Christmas Eve with us (as she has done for the last ten years); as a matter of fact, "Don't expect to see me until spring," she said. Let it be known, however, that she mellowed, and on Christmas Eve morning she called to tell us that she would be gracing us with her presence, that is, if someone could pick her up. Grandma looks wonderful and feels good. I could look forward to being old if I knew that I would have her energy and spunk!

A word about Christmas—it was, at the same time, unsettling and satisfying. I had anticipated leisurely shopping trips with my sisters and Pam (having done all my heavy shopping before

I left home), homemade Christmas tree decorations on a tree that the boys and I had chopped down in the forest, lots of baking and special cooking, and more time than I've ever had to enjoy the season. The picture was not quite that perfect. Most of my time was spent trying to get settled in at Uncle Ed's, and when it became obvious that we would not be living there, I had to move all of our stuff to Mom and Dad's and eventually to Wayne's house. That uncertain and chaotic situation resulted in misplaced items, lost Christmas presents, and constant searching for kids' clothing.

Christmas Eve couldn't have been better. Bill had flown up to be with us so our family was once again complete. After having spent the afternoon up at the hunting cabin watching the kids skate and drink hot chocolate by the gallons, we all met at Gayle and Bill's for appetizers. Then we had dinner at Mom and Dad's (lutefisk and lefse, spareribs, mashed potatoes, glorified rice) followed by coffee and pie and present unwrapping at Pam and Wayne's, an event that took three hours. Presents and wrappings covered the living room but, for some reason, I didn't feel the excessiveness that is overwhelming in other places.

I watched the faces of my sons and wondered if I'll be able to accept the times when they will choose not to spend Christmas with us. How will I feel when they have to share Christmas with their wives' families? Will they adopt different traditions? As a matter of fact, my nieces and nephews will also be scattered someday and have their attention divided. How could there ever be a Christmas without all of them!

On Christmas Day morning we opened presents from Santa Claus and then went to Aunt Millie and Uncle Robert's for dinner. Lucy also accompanied us on that trip and, at one point during the day, she decided that she wanted to go back to the farm, so, unbeknownst to anyone, she left the yard and headed east across the frozen fields. When we realized that she was gone, all of the kids climbed on snocats and caught up with her quite some distance from the house. It was *déjà vu* for all of us, remembering Lucy's rescue from the elements on the way up here and the guilt we felt for not taking care of her.

That evening we opened our family presents under the beautiful little tree that Wayne had chopped down for us and I had decorated with simple ornaments, and then we ate almost all of the Christmas cookies Pam and I had made (those expectations were fulfilled anyway!). Bill, Wayne, and my Bill went into Warroad at about 7:00 to watch the football game with Rod. I stayed home and read Christmas stories to the kids.

I'm always the first to catch the Christmas spirit. And then I love to infuse my home with the joy of the season, wanting to please and insure that everyone is happy. I find it incredible that after forty plus years, I still find the magic in Christmas—year after year, no matter what has preceded it. I love everything about the holiday—even the materialism and the pervasive elevator music, the excessive decorations, the lights, and most especially the age-old Christmas story which I've heard every year since I was born. My excitement starts on November first when the air gets cold and the leaves have left the trees. Then it's suspended until after Thanksgiving because I don't believe in short-changing holidays. Besides, I love Thanksgiving. It's the last calm before the storm, so to speak. The day after Thanksgiving I resume my anticipation of Christmas. It's a wonderfully joyous and generous time, and I feel so sorry for those who are unable or unwilling to find the magic.

On New Years Eve we all left the farm at 4:30 a.m. for two days of skiing at Spirit Mountain in Duluth. The experience was somewhat marred by illnesses: Jon had croup, Katie strep throat, and Rod the flu. But skiing was excellent, and our New Years Eve dinner at the lodge was a large, fun, noisy affair, even though we had to leave Rod in bed. We all had prime rib and, at his request, brought the fat back to Rod who ate it with gusto, flu and all—we were horrified! I don't know what was more hilarious—Rod consuming all that fat with a 102-degree fever, or the kids' mesmerized faces as they watched him smack his lips in anticipation of more! Our family does have a good time being together.

Bill was with us for Christmas and New Years—ten days in all. It felt good to be a family again. The boys especially needed that time together with their Dad. And I didn't fare too badly because Bill and I are always united in wanting to create memorable experiences for our children. It's an unspoken wish: that our children's experiences with family will be so positive that they will want to repeat them with their children.

Sometimes I think I don't know Bill very well anymore. In the early days of our marriage we had a lot in common, but now we see things so differently. Our world views, while once so close together, seem irreconcilable. But I wonder: Is it possible that our differences were always real but we just didn't notice them? Or, are we now choosing to focus on our differences instead of the things that brought us together? It seems that we are increasingly irritated at the idiosyncrasies that we used to find endearing in each other.

Actually, Bill and I are more alike than different in many respects. We're both more introverted than extroverted, for example. But we are wired differently. Bill's a sensor in that he bases his reality in facts and more facts—he tends to focus on what is. I'm an intuitive, intrigued more by the future, by what could be instead of what is. (In fact, I'm willing to forego the facts to right a perceived wrong.) I feel deeply about everything, from animals to nature to people who are hurting in some way. Bill feels deeply about understanding both sides of a picture—always. His unwillingness to take a stand, or make a decision, until he has all of the facts and has analyzed a situation to death is almost legendary. It makes me crazy at times!

Bill comes across as being unemotional and I overly emotional. Neither of us is particularly assertive and certainly not aggressive. I'm more decisive, but my decisions are not always good ones. When Bill gets around to making a decision, it's usually the right one.

One more similarity: Bill and I are both "big picture" people, and we can't accurately remember details, except for those that are related to what each of us considers important. This selective memory causes problems because we argue different details of the same event! We accuse each other of distorting the truth, but it's really a case of not remembering the same things. To further complicate things, I'm often left with impressions, not details, so I can't substantiate my arguments very well. Finally, once I understand an issue, I more often than not, rule with my heart. Bill decides with his head—like the lawyer that he is!

I'm a controlling, stubborn person—more stubborn than controlling, I think, but the effect is the same. Bill isn't like that, and he has to put up with that part of me. I'm sure there are genes for stubbornness, so the trait isn't one that I can easily eliminate from my persona!

I always feel ambivalent on New Years Eve—not wanting the old year to be over, but also feeling excited for a new year to begin. A new year offers hope, of course, but it also promises the unknown—we don't know what's going to happen. Maybe we will learn from our mistakes of the old year, and the new year will be perfect. Maybe my marriage will be perfect! I like the uncertainty.

January 9th—Jon's real birthday! It's hard to believe that my baby is five years old. (Also today Uncle Raymond is 71 and Pat, my father-in-law, is 73.) Jon is such an interesting little guy. Androgynous, with interests that spill into all walks of life and both sexes, his favorite activities are playing school with Roz and Linsay, reading, writing and "helping Grandpa on the farm."

Becoming increasingly conscious of society-perceived gender-appropriate activities, he draws the line at allowing his girl cousins to polish his nails. He continues to be complimentary, very affectionate, and drawn to the aesthetic things in life. Of all my boys, he lavishes affection on me the most, taking advantage of every opportunity to give me a hug and say, "I love you." He crawls into bed with me at night, usually on the nights that he misses Bill, and I don't bother to send him back to his own bed. I asked Mom about the wisdom of that decision, and she told me not to worry, that I shouldn't deprive him of the security he must need at this time in his life.

Today Jon is his usual happy self, and one would never know from his behavior that he was depressed last night. But I know—and I feel guilty for intentionally exposing him to the pain of missing his father. What gives me the right to do that to my son?

Roseau wasted Warroad in hockey last night (9-0). What a brouhaha that was! For the last three years Warroad has edged out Roseau, and this year Rams fans turned out in droves to see the tables turned. It was no contest; the Rams played games with the Warriors on the ice, making them look like pawns in a chess game. The arena was packed with fans from both sides, with a hundred outside waiting for a square foot of standing space. The roar of the crowd for every goal was deafening. The Roseau fans were obnoxious; the Warroad fans meek. And so the rivalry continues.

Wayne doesn't think he got the administrative job he applied for at Marvin's. Ironically, he thinks that his forthrightness cost him a position that has prestige, challenges and, best of all, daylight hours (no more night shifts). During his second interview, he told Conrad Marvin that he had a beef herd which was of primary importance to him and that, while he didn't mind arriving at work as early as 4:30 a.m. and foregoing lunch, he would like to leave the office most days at 2:30 in order to do farm chores. I guess that proposal wasn't acceptable. It would never occur to Wayne to be anything but honest and out front with people; his high moral standards preclude any ethical lapse. Sometimes I think he's too hard on himself and, maybe, even on others he loves. But he would, as the saying goes, give you the shirt off his back.

One of the most poignant memories of my brother comes from a letter he wrote to me in Toledo in 1976 while he was studying carpentry at Northland College. I had just begun my job at The University of Toledo and was still suffering the pangs of separation from Bill, so a letter from anyone was welcome, but especially from my brother who doesn't write often.

I remember the details of that letter well. It began with the announcement that he didn't have to frame houses that day because it was MEA and students had a couple of days off. It was cold and he had a touch of pneumonia so he was glad for the respite. During his time off he helped Dad build another shack for the cattle and a well house for his uncle. He went on to describe the disappointment he was feeling because the DNR hadn't opened up deer hunting season yet, and there was no reason to start up the old car and roam down old hunting roads with Dad, a pastime that he looks forward to every year.

At that point, Wayne stated that it was time to get down to business: He had a favor to ask. He wanted to ask Pam to marry him and he had a plan for giving her an engagement ring. He was going to make arrangements at Lon's, a high-class restaurant in Thief River, to have everything set up for a dinner for two. He was going to buy one long-stemmed rose and have that in the middle of the table. After they ate, his plan was to ask Lon to play "Color My World" on the stereo system. Halfway through the song, the waiter would bring the ring over and Wayne would present it to Pam. Now here's where I came in. In light of the fact that I have good handwriting, Wayne wanted to know if I would write the words to the song on fancy paper and make two copies so that both he and Pam could have the words by their placemats while they listened. He wrote down the words for me: *As time goes on, I realize what you mean to me. And now, now that you're near, promise your love, that I've waited to share. And dream of our moments together. Color my world with hopes of loving you.*

Wayne ended the letter with a word of thanks. He said that he was really excited about doing this, and Pam didn't have the slightest idea about any of this, so he thought it should be all right. And indeed it was.

Three

Wonders of all wonders—school was cancelled yesterday! We had a blizzard with lots of wind but minimal snow, and the roads were clear so no one could understand the cancellation. Katie and Linsay were stunned! Katie exclaimed, "Last year, when it was forty below and tons of snow, we had to walk halfway to Moser's to meet the bus, but they wouldn't cancel school!" The boys had a wonderful time—read, practiced the piano, and wrote letters in the morning and played outside building tunnels and forts all afternoon. Willie went snocatting with Chris and Robert Moser for a while. All of the kids watched a movie at Gayle's until suppertime.

My day was fun also. After the first hectic hour of the morning, when darling Hannah required attention, Jon and Roz clamored for breakfast, and the older kids tramped back home after the bus had failed to pick them up, Wayne and I planned our family trip out West this summer. Mom, who had gone to school at 6:15 as usual, unaware of the cancellation, was finally picked up at 11:00, and then she and Dad entered into our discussion. I've discovered that one thing Wayne and I have in common is our enjoyment of planning and anticipating family vacations. We pour over maps and brochures with relish and unabashed enthusiasm.

I love to take care of little Hannah on Thursdays and Fridays. She is a sweet and happy baby—so cute with her big blue eyes and cotton candy hair. Sometimes I think that the happiest moments of my life were the beginnings of each of my boys' lives, when they were babies and my most important responsibility was taking care of them. Daily rides with them all bundled up in the little red wagon provided me with infinite happiness.

My days have settled into a routine of sorts—one that fills me with such contentment, I refuse to think about the future, especially the end of my stay here. The other day, for example, Joyce and Jena came out for dinner and then we went to town to watch Willie play basketball and Zach hockey. That night everyone climbed into the van to watch Roseau beat Grand Forks in hockey. I remember thinking that life couldn't possibly get any better!

During that week of bitterly cold and virtually snowless weather before Christmas, the pipes froze at Mom and Dad's. We were living with them at the time, and, for several days, we alternated between having no hot water and having no water period. We carried water from Wayne's and heated it on the stove to bathe and do dishes. The toilet didn't work, so we had to make frequent trips to his bathroom. Some of us chose to use the old outside toilet for nostalgic reasons. Still furnished with back issues of Sears and Montgomery Wards catalogs, it conjures up memories of the olden days, when Joyce and I wouldn't drink anything after 6 o'clock for fear that we'd have to make a nocturnal trip in the frigid hours of darkness. The catalogs provided opportunities for daydreaming about wonderful items that had little chance of ever being purchased, but the possibilities made the cold sojourn a lot more palatable.

Contrary to expectations, there was little hardship during that period of adversity, only minor inconvenience. Rod, Bill, Wayne, my Bill, and Dad worked outside in that subzero cold until finally, after numerous failed attempts, got the pipes working.

The kids thought of the whole episode as an adventure (although they wouldn't have anything to do with the outdoor toilet) and helped carry the water with little complaining. At one point, though, I heard Zach say to Linsay, "If you carry my pail, I'll pull you five times on the sled."

Linsay countered with "Uh uh, Zach, that's not enough."

"Yes it is," said Zach, "but I'll also let you be on my side when we play King of the Hill." He finally conned Linsay into carrying his pail, which she did until she got tired, and then she just left it on the path where the water froze and had to be thawed out before it could be used. I never did find out if Zach kept his end of the bargain.

The weather warmed on Christmas Eve and we've had no trouble since then. It was a hectic but very satisfying time when all of us worked together to solve a problem—reminiscent of the olden days when problems of this nature cropped up often. I suspect that those who live up here and have to deal with frozen pipes pretty often think I'm strange for romanticizing the situation. I do that often: lapse into a 1940s fog when I listen to my parents' stories—the hardships they endured, the hand-to-mouth living, making do with the barest of necessities—and all I can think of is how relatively simple life was then. Hard? Yes, definitely. But it was a simpler world—fewer demands, choices, decisions to be made. Happiness flowed from a weariness that came from working hard to keep your family intact—healthy and happy. They just had to have been good times—the olden days.

As time goes by, I'm entertaining thoughts of not resuming my university career. I don't miss the university and have no interest in pursuing reading research during my sabbatical. There! I've said it! My day-to-day happiness is now so complete that I have difficulty even considering the addition of another dimension to my life. I might still observe Mom's classroom at Malung School and write my article, but I don't think I'll get much else done in the way of academic achievement. While my main interests at this point are parenting and home management, I'd like to find something else that would be part-time, lucrative and satisfying when I get home. Writing is an option that would fulfill two of the three requirements, but I really do want to make some money—it doesn't have to be a lot—so that I'm not totally dependent upon Bill. I've always tried to pay my own way, or at least assume some measure of financial independence, even all those years in college and graduate school when I had almost no money.

Has it really been fifteen years since I left Bill standing on a street corner so that I could pursue my career in another state? The moment was so vividly implanted in my brain that I can still call to mind every detail.

Bill had one more year of law school when I finished my PhD in 1976, and we were faced with two choices: both stay in Minneapolis where I would find a job unrelated to my degree (the University of Minnesota wouldn't hire its own graduates) while Bill finished law school, or live apart for a year so I could accept an academic position at another university. We chose the latter option. At the time, it hadn't seemed difficult to make that decision, but now that we had to separate—I had been offered a job at The University of Toledo—we wondered if we had made the right one.

We packed up everything I owned and needed in rust-riddled old Petunia, my 1966 Dodge Cornet, and I drove Bill to the St. Paul law firm where he was working as an intern. He got out of the car on the street corner by his office and we said our goodbye. I watch him while driving away, waving until I was out of sight. And then the tears flowed. I could not breathe for the heaviness pressing against my chest. My heart was literally damaged—I could feel it tearing apart. I loved him so much, and not even the anticipation of a new adventure could allay the fear that I would not be good at anything without him. I wanted to yell, "I can't go. I depend upon you too much. You're the center of my world—my calm harbor—my intellectual guide!" I cried all the way to Chicago.

I remember a letter I received from Bill a couple of days after my departure. I memorized the beginning: "Dearest Judy, a letter of firsts—the first letter of our separation written the first day thereof; probably the first letter you'll get at your first real job; finally, maybe the first letter addressed to you with your new title." It ended with an admonition to "do a number" on my job ("Dr. Patberg") and a reminder that I really am the greatest and shouldn't let anyone have the slightest hesitation about that. I felt so good about myself and a lot better about our separation. Bill always seems to be able to accomplish that even today. He builds me up when I need it. Sometimes this need is so great that I think life was provisional until I met Bill. Everything up to that point was a question mark.

Anyway, I did do well. Along with my feelings of uprootedness and mild confusion about some of the precise aspects of my role was a confidence that I possessed everything I needed to be a professor. I had been well-trained in my doctoral program, so I immediately felt comfortable in my role as a definer, a framer-of-ideas (an intellectually tidy one). I enjoyed feeling my way. I did not find any aspect of my job dull and kept terribly busy. When I felt discomfort with the newness and structural ambiguity of things, I reminded myself who I was—that I was competent, that I possessed the knowledge and expertise my department needed. So I hung loose and learned all that there was to learn as quickly as I could. Then gradually, but insistently, I interposed my opinions, my views, my exceptions and additions and observations—all of which were taken seriously.

What has happened to make me say I don't want to resume my career at The University of Toledo? I could say that most of the important ideas have been defined and framed, and the job has ceased to be as interesting and challenging as it once was so I'm no longer thriving, but I think I'm just feeling restless and want a change. Maybe fifteen years at any job would result in the same feeling. I'll have to do some more thinking about this.

Willie's basketball game was cancelled on Friday night. We were all disappointed, but we went to Hardy's and caught the third period of the Roseau hockey game that was proceeding in the usual manner—the Rams slaughtering their opponent, in this case, East Grand Forks. Roseau is so good this year that it is tempting to think of them not only going to State but winning the title!

Mom, Katie and I went with Gayle to Grygla for Jenny's basketball game on Saturday, while all of the boys and Linsay stayed home to snocat and work on their fort. Jon and Rozie wanted to stay home with Pam. It was a lazy day—fun, but nothing concrete accomplished. It's still hard for me to completely relax and enjoy doing nothing, probably because I have so much to do, or rather so much that I think I should do, that I feel I need to do—when really, I don't have to do much of anything.

Jenny played only 30 seconds in her game, which Roseau won handily, giving them the tournament championship. I felt so bad for her because all of us had come to see her play. Jenny was a star basketball player in the 7th and 8th grades and now, as a freshman, she hasn't been playing much. The new coach doesn't hold her in the same high regard that her old coach held her, because Jenny couldn't attend basketball camp over the summer, having to spend the months in Wyoming with her mother instead. Even if it were the case that Jenny lost her edge over the summer, I was once again reminded of how wrong competitive sports can be if the coach is more interested in the game score than in the kids. In this case, as in so many, the coach was not satisfied just to win; she had to compile as many points as possible. Consequently, four girls played little or not at all. If she had staggered their playing she still would have won the game. When I saw how frustrated and upset Jenny was, the whole event left a sour taste in my mouth. If I were a coach, winning could never be as important as a child's happiness. With that attitude, I'll probably never be a coach!

Sunday was another wonderful day from beginning to end. After church we met Joyce and Rod, et al. at Mom and Dad's and devoured homemade vegetable soup with dumplings. All of us then proceeded up to Bemis Hill via snocats and pickup where we sledded with the kids. At 3:30 we snocatted over to the hunting cabin and had a supper of spaghetti, cake, cookies, apples, garlic bread, coffee, and hot chocolate. While we were there, the kids took turns driving the new snocat in the field, accompanied by an adult. Willie would like to be given permission to drive the snocat whenever he wants to, but we won't allow it yet, so he has to settle for driving it with an adult. I think that Willie must have set Chris and Jenny up because they both came to me with their most innocent faces and said, "Auntie Judy, Willie does a good job of driving the snocat. He doesn't even go very fast, so you should let him drive it." Ah, huh. I must say though that all of the evidence thus far suggests that he will be a responsible and cautious driver, so it probably won't be long before he's allowed to drive it alone.

The winter activities were fun, but what made the day special was the company. With the exception of Gayle, Bill and Tony (Tony had a hockey game in Baudette) we were all together. Whatever else can be said about our family, we enjoy each other's company more than anyone else's. My siblings and in-laws are my best friends and I like being with them. Our spouses like to compare notes on the Pearson girls and spend time analyzing us, focusing on our faults which, at one time or another, have the following labels: opinionated, stubborn, single-minded, willful, directive, controlling and assertive (or aggressive, depending on whether they want to praise or damn!). Although Pam is not involved in these conversations, I have the feeling that she would describe Wayne in the same way. The "outlaws" maintain that their analyses are all in fun—and they are, I guess—but this kind of character sketch is unfair in its one-sidedness. We Pearsons are also extremely loyal and generous, kind, affectionate, loving, industrious, nurturing, and faithful. These qualities ought to count at least as much as the more negative ones!

That evening we watched a home video show on television and laughed until our sides hurt. We agreed that we probably had award-winning video scenes all around us and, to prove our point, Wayne called his dog Charlie over to his chair and began howling. Soon Charlie joined in and they howled in unison. They even looked alike! The whole scene was funnier than anything we saw on TV.

Jon missed his Dad again at bedtime, and when I reminded him of the birthday card Bill had sent, he immediately ran off to find the special box he kept it in. He could not find the box and was so sad. Just when it seemed that his doldrums couldn't get any worse, I dropped the ceramic Mickey Mouse music box I gave him for Christmas and it smashed into smithereens. His wail turned into serious sobbing and I felt low—not only didn't he have his Daddy, but now he no longer had the special present from me that reminded him of his Dad.

"I just don't understand," he moaned, "how this could happen when I feel so sad already."

I tried to reassure him that it could be replaced but he was inconsolable. "You can't replace it; it's broken—see it's all on the floor," he kept repeating.

Finally, I went to bed with him and sang him nursery rhymes and Peace Corps songs until he eventually went to sleep. Jon is as happy as he can be 95 percent of the time and unhappy the rest of the time only because he misses Bill—mostly at night. It breaks my heart to see him so sad, and I invariably feel guilty for creating the separation.

The next morning, his first thought was to find his box—which Rozie did after searching for a while. Jon retrieved his card, asked me to read it to him, and put it under his pillow.

"There," he said, "now I can touch it when I miss Daddy at night. Read it to me once more, Mommy." I pulled it out from under the pillow and read it again: "Dear Jon, Happy Birthday! I can't believe you're already five years old. I guess you're not my baby anymore. Daddy is very proud of you. You are a special little, I mean BIG boy and I love you a lot. Love, Daddy."

After I finished reading, Jon's face lit up and he ran off to see what Rozie was doing. When she saw him coming, she couldn't resist telling him, "Jon, you know I found your box so you could be happy (hands on hips)."

"Yeah, yeah, yeah, I know, Rozie, good for you!" he said.

"Ya, well then, and so; hello, good day and hello; who loves Grandpa?; blast off to (Thief River, Warroad); long day—short day; Hannah's the name and tough is her game; shit town (Roseau) and boom town (Warroad); better start believing it—favorite sayings of my Dad. Sixty-four years old and retired from the lumberjack business, his preferred colors are brown and tan, and his favorite activities include: unhurried trips to Thief River, ice fishing, reading non-fiction, spending time in libraries, taking care of grandchildren (must be toilet-trained), discussing politics (left-wing liberal with conservative social values), traveling ("see the country"), feeding the birds (red poles, nut hatches, snow birds, sparrows, blue jays, and yellow and red gross beaks, which are the "King of the Winter Birds"), snocatting, and watching news and human interest programs along with his favorite shows—*Matlock, Murder She Wrote, Island Sun* and *Unsolved Mysteries*. He dislikes Morris the cat, conservative politicians, fiction, wind, fundamentalist

Christians with narrow minds, people with an unfounded fear of communism, pollution, television shows and books containing swear words, debt, and having to watch television from anywhere but his chair on the left of the sofa. He is kind, humorous, nice-looking, concerned about his personal appearance, hard-working, stubborn, inflexible, flexible, opinionated, argumentative, an avid reader, politically aware, and interesting. He relates well with grandchildren, possesses a strong love of family, and enjoys family outings (but not large extended family gatherings). He relishes the role of devil's advocate and clashes with Wayne on how to run the farm. (Author's note: See *We Just Shoveled Two Feet of Partly Cloudy* for memories and biographical information.)

I think that politics turned really personal in our last election. Mike Dukakis had a 20 percent lead over Bush because of the way Dukakis had turned Massachusetts's economy around when he was governor. But then Bush's advisors dug into Dukakis's history and found out that he had released Willie Horton, a black convicted murderer, from jail as part of the pardon program. Horton then raped a white woman; Bush accused Dukakis of being weak on crime; and, incredibly, Dukakis refused to accuse the Bush campaign of being racist. Bush capitalized on this—kept running the Horton ads—and Dukakis won the presidency for Bush. Even in competition with the bumbling Dukakis campaign and the advantage of money and incumbency, Bush managed to eke out only a slight margin. Only 49% of the voters turned out to vote. It was pitiful. His presidency so far is pitiful also. The "thousand points of light" he pledged for volunteerism and his promise to avoid war—both have become a joke in irreverent circles, as has his vice president, Dan Quayle. What is the matter with us that we could allow such incompetent people to run our country? My dislike and disdain are pretty intense at times.

The decades seem to be flying by. I still mourn the loss of Martin Luther King and the Kennedys, especially Bobby. Their names symbolize unfulfilled dreams and promises, and I ache for what our country might be like today if they had lived—what might have been. I try to ignore stories about the Kennedys' private lives, and regret that their reputations are being tarnished for future generations.

Four

This has been the most unbelievable winter! The days have been mild (20 to 30 degrees). It snows enough to keep the snocats going and make the world beautiful but there has, as yet, been no accumulation to hamper activities. Sunshine and dripping icicles almost every day contribute greatly to one's well-being.

Speaking of well-being, the boys and I spent a quiet and euphoric week-end at the hunting shack (*Jakt Stuga*) located on the edge of the woods just north of the house. It was so peaceful and relaxing I regretted having to return to normal living on Sunday night. Someone once said that, because life is complicated, we need to find a place where peace and simplicity calm us down. For me, that place is the farm and, even more so, the hunting shack.

The adventure began on Friday night when I visited with Grandma Rosie while Willie and Zach went to a movie with Chris and Tony. Jon and Roz stayed home with Mom and Dad because, as Jon said, "We don't get to spend enough time with Grandma, Mommy." He went on to describe all of the things they did with Grandpa during the day—with Roz nodding her head, encouraging him to continue—and then finished with a flourish, "so you see, Mommy, we're going to let Grandma do things with us tonight." Rozie patted him on the arm and said, "Good job, Jon." I could hardly stand it—they were so sincere!

Anyway, after the movie, the boys and I headed for home, hastily packed Wayne's pickup with food and minimal clothing, and arrived at the cabin at 11:30. We stayed up playing games until 12:30 during which time Willie consumed a huge amount of chips and salsa.

The next morning we awakened to the sound of a snocat which Mom and Wayne brought out for us to use. We all had coffee at 9:15 and then Zachie and I rode over to Grandma's so he could practice the piano. Willie was supposed to do that also but he had stomach problems (chips and salsa?) and spent most of the morning hanging his head over a kettle that curiously stayed dry! When I asked Zach how he thought practice had gone, he said, "Well, I know Grandma liked to listen to me play, but I don't think Grandpa did because he kept saying, 'That's good now, Zach.'"

We returned to the camp to find Joyce and Rod waiting for us; they were there to pick up Jon and Roz who were going to spend the afternoon with them. Gayle, Bill and the kids stopped by so we had a full house. It was fun shooting the breeze in those cramped quarters.

On Saturday night Chris and Tony stayed with us, and the noise level rose considerably. The boys built tunnels in the drifts in the pond and played Hide and Go Seek. We roasted marshmallows over a bonfire that also consumed pop cans, paper plates and anything else the kids found to throw away. Tired from his afternoon in Warroad without a nap, Jon fought to be competitive, but couldn't quite keep up and finally succumbed to sleep around 10:00. Actually, all of us were sleeping by 11:00 and woke up at 7:30 on Sunday morning. Tony and Chris left to go to church, so once again we were alone. After awhile, we snocatted to the farm for a visit and then proceeded to Bemis Hill with Dad, Mom, Wayne, Katie, Linsay, and Rozie. Mom let Willie drive the snocat all the way to Bemis Hill, and he couldn't refrain from chastising me a little. "Grandma trusts me, Mom, and she knows a lot more about snocatting than you do, so you should let me drive by myself now." Well, I felt chastened enough to assure him that I would think it over.

When we returned, we played outside, read, and ate leftovers. At 6:30 we cleaned up, packed, took one last spin around the field and returned to the farm. The first item on our agenda was a shower.

It was an idyllic week-end. We ate when we were hungry and slept when we were tired. We wound up the old clock, not to keep track of the time, but to be comforted by the soft sound breaking an even softer silence. It was a delicious taste of a past life. It was exactly the kind of experience for the boys that contributed to my decision to move up here for four months. It gave them first-hand experience with an outdoor toilet and lanterns that cast a soft glow around the small cabin. The boys loved the lanterns but the outdoor toilet left them cold—literally. When Zach first saw the deluxe model his Uncle Wayne had built (cover on the seat and a Plexiglas window), he exclaimed, "Awesome, totally awesome!" Then reality set in, and he insisted he couldn't sit down because the seat had frost on it. His sojourn was very short.

Jonathan "held it" until Sunday when he made a mad dash out of the cabin without saying anything to anyone. Before I knew what was going on, we heard a blood-curdling scream. We all ran outside fearing that he had fallen in. It turned out that he had not pulled his pants down all the way and had practically filled his boots! He was already hysterical so I couldn't be angry—anyway, it was my fault for not going with him to show him how to do it the outdoor way. Poor little guy!

It was with sad reluctance we said goodbye to the hunting cabin. Even though we were aware that another stay was likely before we returned home, it would not be the same as this one. I firmly believe that this was one experience the boys will never forget because it was so different from all the rest. The only void in our lives during the weekend was Bill. We talked about him and speculated on how he would have enjoyed the experience. Each of us missed him in our own way.

The hunting shack is a reminder of how little it takes to get by and how wonderful it is not to have to think about anything else. I wanted to stay but I couldn't without my husband.

Just thinking about Bill reminded me of how we met so many years ago. When my Peace Corps experience terminated in May of 1972, I used my transition allowance to travel around Southeast Asia. I ended up in Petchburi, Thailand where I met a Peace Corps Volunteer named Bill Patberg. I stayed in Petchburi for two weeks and then had to leave because my visa expired. I couldn't get it renewed, so I made a side trip to Nepal and almost finished a trek to the base camp at Mount Everest. When I came down from the mountains, there was an invitation from Bill waiting for me at the Peace Corps office in Kathmandu. He wanted me to come back.

I caught the next plane back to Bangkok, having sold everything I owned, including my rucksack, in order to purchase a plane ticket (and still had to beg the airlines to make up the difference). This time I stayed in Petchburi for about a month (again, visa length) and it was one of the most wonderful, happiest months I've ever known. We didn't do very much really, except get to know each other. We went swimming, enjoyed moonlight rides on his motorcycle, and ate a lot. I helped Bill type his lesson plans and watched him teach. We participated in a Buddhist ordination. But most of all, we laughed, sang and even danced a little—thoroughly enjoying each other. Eventually, we fell in love. There was no debate, no frustration, no agony of yes/no, no mixed emotions. Bill was everything I'd been looking for and I was happy. I felt more comfortable, calm and self-confident with him than I ever had with any other person. Even when I was petty or angry, or he disagreed or was angry with me, there was something else, something different that wasn't touched by any of those reactions. It was as if there was something between us that was rock solid and unshakable, and it remained there unaffected by anger, disagreement, disappointment, mood, or anything else. I was confident that if I were wrong and he knew it and the whole world condemned me, he might condemn me too, but there would always be that thing beneath it all by which he would choose me wrong rather than the whole world right. I suppose you would call that love, but it didn't fit any conception of the word that I'd ever had.

And yet, through all this in our time together, we remained separate—different people with different ideas and beliefs, and we were able to enjoy and appreciate each other not in spite of, but because of, our differences. A metaphor in *The Prophet* kept popping up during that time: Lovers should be like strings on a lyre—each with separate notes and qualities but when one is plucked, the other vibrates sympathetically.

So what happened? Eighteen years later, sixteen for which we've been married, Bill and I are angry with each other too much of the time and our marriage is marked by turbulence. I wonder if it's so different from the marriage hassles that seem to be cropping up with such frequency today—probably due in large part to the terrible rate at which we are bombarded with new people, new ideas, new opportunities, and new things. I remember reading *Future Shock* while I was in the Peace Corps. The book talks about the shattering stress and disorientation people suffer from because of too much change in too short a time. It seems as if we're always changing ourselves and our world.

If people are not careful, even when they are living together, they can wake up some morning and find that all of this newness has conspired to create two individuals who have changed in idea and approach to such an extent that they don't know each other any more. If Bill and I were dating instead of married, we could simply move apart and follow the strongest of our desires and influences. However, we are married and this fact at times produces unhappiness, grief, repercussions and upsets which would never have been without the "I dos." But other generations (e.g., my parents) have made it, and certainly the factors of new influences and experiences existed in the past, producing change in both people and straining the marriage. I think, however, that the marriage bond is strained even more today with the unprecedented bombardment of experiences, both real and vicarious, which forces people to change significantly, rapidly, and unalterably. When this happens, that fragile little thing called love disappears.

Perhaps it is true, then, that a marriage contract which is expected to last "till death do us part" is really an anachronism—a throwback from an age of slower change and more permanence. Possibly it is truly unrealistic to expect that two people should maintain an unflagging interest in each other for 50 years (or even 18).

When you think about it, marriage vows make no sense because two people are promising themselves to the unknown person each will become in the future, e.g., twenty years later. The person you married can be so different as to be almost unrecognizable. Outsiders like to urge couples whose marriages are in trouble to examine the reasons they married their spouse in the first place. But, what if those reasons no longer exist? What if, after 16 years of marriage, they are growing apart and are, in many ways, different people from who they were when they got married? I know that many of the problems we are having derive from a determination on my part to get from Bill what I want, what I think I need, instead of being happy with what he can give me. I admit to insisting that he should change, but why should my way be superior to his way? Why does marriage have to be so hard? If it were easier would it be any less good?

I love Bill and I'm going to try very hard to accept the limits of our marriage—no, embrace them, for they force me to focus on all that is right and good about our marriage instead of those things I can't have. I cherish the idea of one lifelong relationship with one person.

Those marriages that do survive—and I want to believe that ours will be one of them—have to be made that much closer and that much more meaningful to both people, for their lives must not only join in bed but in every waking and sleeping hour. "Intercourse" in its original meaning has to be maintained continuously "like two strings on a harp—separate but vibrating sympathetically."

There seems to be a pattern in our relationship: during the good times, we celebrate the day we met; during the bad times, we rue that day.

I miss Bill, but then I always miss him and think about him in the most loving ways when we're apart.

Yesterday we awoke to find three inches of new snow on the ground. The world was brilliant. Dad and I were childless, so we drove the snocats all around the Bemis Hill area in virgin snow through the sparkling evergreen and stately birch forest. Slowly maneuvering the narrow trails in the forest, and then feeling the cold wind on my face while racing through the wide-open fields made me feel very young and vibrant again. It was an exhilarating time!

I've begun a nightly ritual with the kids. As soon as they get ready for bed they all pile into the two bunk beds and eagerly await the latest installment in my past adventures. Breathless and wide-eyed, they listen while I recount my experiences as a Peace Corps Volunteer in the Philippines and during my travels in Southeast Asia. They also clamor for stories about "when you were young, Mom/Auntie Judy." My boys have already heard most of my world adventure tales but they don't seem to tire of them and are eager to hear them again with their cousins.

One of their favorite stories is about an experience I had returning to Thailand from Nepal because I desperately wanted to see Bill. I flew into Bangkok and had to get to Petchburi where Bill was teaching. The problem was I had no money for a bus, so I decided to hitchhike. As soon as I sat down in the first car that stopped, I knew that I shouldn't have accepted the ride. The man started caressing my leg and saying things in Thai that I'm sure I wouldn't have wanted to hear in English. I didn't panic until he stopped at a little road side hotel and ordered me out of the car, making sure that I saw the gun that was prominently displayed in his pants. He opened the door to a musty, dimly lit room and pushed me inside. He strategically and noisily placed his gun on the dresser beside the door and gestured for me to take off my clothes and lie down. I pretended to obey, and my response must have made him overly confident because he took his eyes off me and moved to the other side of the bed. I knew this would be my only chance, so I grabbed the gun and ran out the door toward the road where there was a bus waiting for passengers to disembark. The man ran after me, but when I flung the gun on the ground, he stopped to pick it up and didn't resume his pursuit. At first the driver wouldn't let me on the bus without any *baht*, but I must have pleaded my case convincingly because he eventually told me to sit down. I rode all the way to Petchburi, surrounded by people, chickens and pigs.

When I arrived at the bus garage in Petchburi, I had another moment of panic because I still had no money, and therefore no way to get out to the Teachers College where Bill lived. Once again, I had to resort to other measures, and the idea that came to me was so absurd that even I didn't think it would work. But it did. I handed the rickshaw driver a piece of paper with I.O.U written in large letters on it and asked him for a ride to the Teachers College. He complied and, by the way, I made good on that I.O.U before I left Petchburi.

After a dusty, bumpy, embarrassing ride (I outweighed the little guy by thirty pounds!) I arrived at Bill's house only to find him not at home. A neighbor, seeing me pounding on the door, ran over to tell me that Bill was in Bangkok for the weekend! I had to break into his house. He found me the next day, sleeping and covered with bedbug bites and reactions to the bites (remnants from my Nepal trek)—a pathetic sight indeed.

The kids love this story—the absurdity of the situation, first of all, and then the question of how the man could have thought I was pretty enough to want to be with me, given the presence of my body bites. Linsay said, "He must not have had a lot of girlfriends, Auntie Judy."

Today I was thinking—again!—about relationships, marriage, love, and transience. I have a nagging suspicion that, while all of those concepts have been present in past generations, there's something different about the way they affect our lives today. I think about women in my parents' generation who waited three, four, five years for husbands and boyfriends who were serving in World War II. I don't think that that kind of patience and endurance on a large scale is possible today. Even if it were, what are the chances that a relationship can successfully be picked up again after that kind of separation? I submit that those chances are considerably fewer today than they were in my parents' generation.

Couples who are divorced, getting divorced, separated or otherwise having marital problems are the norm today. What is remarkable is a couple who doesn't fit somehow into that schema. With the divorce rate somewhere around 40 % and the whole institution of marriage under attack—with trial marriages, contract marriages, communes, five- and ten-year marriages, etc. springing up everywhere—I think it's a demonstrable fact that love doesn't last as long as it used to, at least when we talk about the kind of love that causes people to form a long-term, extremely close relationship.

What this short-term love (and love it is—no one goes through the legal hassle of getting married if he expects to separate later, so he must have been in love initially) forbodes in terms of morality, whether it will bring increased independence or merely increased decadence, is largely a matter of opinion. What I think is the more important question is what this transience indicates about the conditions of society now and in the immediate future and the changes we have to make in our views and values in order to cope. Bemoaning the fact is useless. This is the way it is, and probably not the way it should be—and we can only blame ourselves for that.

So, we have but two choices: to cope and participate—accepting the inevitable—or isolate ourselves and try to ignore it. Both are viable alternatives, but the former seems to be the healthier and more productive. When I say we should accept the inevitable, I'm not saying we should buckle under or concede our values. There is always the alternative of fighting. But, at least in the short run, that seems to be a little hopeless, and the present situation will almost certainly demand certain changes of attitude in order to fight realistically.

If people are finding themselves increasingly unable to stay in love for a long period of time, then what does that say about families? Obviously, their durational expectancy is way down, for a family is founded on little else than love. And if the family—that very symbol of permanence, grounding, and stability—is itself being uprooted, indeed toppled, what does it say about the extent to which transience has rooted itself in our society? If the family is becoming "transient" (in the sense of passing) what chance has friendship? Obviously, many of our ideas on interpersonal relations are going to have to be rethought and re-evaluated. Some of them will go down very hard. But again it seems to be a matter of sink or swim.

I don't think this transience is a passing thing. It is not something that can simply be endured. It is something that is basic to the psyche of the people. People today don't expect things to last. Have you heard the comment that we live in a throwaway culture? I'm using a pen that cost me ten cents and if I think it doesn't write well, I simply will throw it away. Did anyone in my parents' generation ever consider throwing a pen away because it didn't produce good penmanship? Likewise, the object of much ridicule and complaining is planned obsolescence. But people want it. Volvo will never sell well in America because it brags of lasting 11 years—not terribly long—but Chevrolet sells fantastically well because it advertises a "new" model every six to eight months. People don't want the same car for 11 years—that would be boring. We think that things should change quickly. I think about the emphasis that advertising puts on words like "new," "improved," "better," all of which indicate that the old product is somehow inferior. Whatever you say about advertising it is, generally speaking, telling people what they want to hear.

People don't want things to be permanent. I don't think it's just the new generation. That's too facile. The idea is increasing with time but not along generational lines.

What I do think is that the casualty of transience that is the most overwhelmingly depressing is the idea that people don't expect relationships to last. The demands on our time that today's life puts on us, the opportunities that it presents, are so myriad and so pressing that we literally don't have time for friends who aren't in easy reach. Well, I guess that's enough philosophizing for now.

I met Bill's parents in a most unorthodox manner. While we were together in Thailand, Bill wrote a letter of introduction to his parents, informing them of my existence in his life. I took it home with me when I left Thailand. Upon landing in New York,

I didn't have enough money for a taxi to his parents' house in New Jersey and I was tired, so I slept in the airport with my bag chained to the bench. The next morning, a cab driver woke me up and asked me where I needed to go. I explained my dilemma, and he said that he was going that way and would give me a ride. So there I was—standing on Bill's parents' doorstep, bearing greetings and a letter of introduction from Bill. I never read the letter so I don't know what he said, but it must have been good enough for his parents to not only take me in, but host a party for me a couple of days later. I ended up staying with them for a week instead of the intended two days. Their hospitality was generous beyond belief. However, I don't think I'm living up to the expectations of what Bill's mother wanted for her son. If Bill hadn't married me, he most likely would have been a high-powered lawyer in New York or Washington, D.C.

I like it when Katie, Linsay, Willie and Zach all come home on the school bus together. It happens two nights a week when no one has sports practice or church activities. They all trudge over to Mom and Dad's for homemade cornbread and then Dad, Wayne and I take them for snocat rides or they play outside. They watch a little television, practice the piano (sometimes) and then just generally fool around before going to bed. The boys like those nights also; sometimes I think they'd rather have evenings at home every night then go to practice. In fact, I won't be surprised if Willie decides to quit basketball. He vacillates between having fun with the boys on the team and wishing that all of his time was free to play with his cousins. When Chris, Jenny and Tony come over in the evening, the noise level is pretty high and things can get a little out of control, but they all have so much fun together that Pam and I clean up the mess without grousing too much. We think that the bonding that's taking place now, when they are so young, will stay with them forever. I hope we're not wrong about that.

The other day the kids were all outside playing "King of the Hill" on the snow banks, and Katie came running into the house, all breathless and covered with snow. "Auntie Judy," she said, "you have to come out! Me and Linsay and Jenny are keeping the boys off the hill!" I don't know exactly why, but watching the kids play made me feel a kind of poignant sadness for children in the future. I have this feeling that my boys and my nieces and nephews are the last generation to enjoy unstructured play, because technology will increasingly dictate what children do during their free time. I wonder if my grandchildren will play "King of the Hill" and build indoor forts with refrigerator boxes and blankets the way these kids do.

Both boys are being harassed at school these days and the only reason I can think of is that they're the new kids on the block and territorial rights have to be protected. One boy, in particular, makes life difficult for them by acting like the classic bully. When Zach got home from school one day he said, "Mom, I did what you told me to do. I tried to be nice to Mike when I saw him at the skating rink. I told him that I had missed him the last couple of days and you know what he did? Picked me up by the ears and slammed me into the boards!" Apparently, Zach then called Mike a jerk and gave him a shove. When I asked him what happened then, he said, "He never moved much. He's really big!" Zach seems to be able to deal with the situation, especially since Mike isn't in his grade and he has Tony and his friends for allies.

Willie, on the other hand, is having a tougher time because Mike is in his class. During the first two weeks of school, I kept getting reports about how popular Will was and he, himself, felt that he had made a number of friends. Then I don't know what happened, but I think that Mike became jealous of Willie's popularity and turned on him. He also turned other kids against him. For example, Matt, who was Willie's best friend in the beginning, suddenly became his enemy and would do hurtful things such as not tell Willie when basketball practice was.

One day when I was at Malung to give a presentation on my trip to the Soviet Union, I heard Willie ask Matt about basketball practice. Matt just ignored him so when Willie left, I went up to Matt and asked him the same question. He answered me and when I asked him why he didn't answer Will, he shrugged. That little intervention exacerbated an already bad situation in that Matt told everyone at basketball practice that Will had to have his mother solve his problems for him. Poor Willie—he was mortified and asked me to please not interfere anymore. Well, I did (much to my chagrin now)—one more time. I called Matt's mother (whom I knew from high school), briefly explained what was happening at school, and asked if I could meet her someplace to discuss the problem. When I arrived at our meeting place, she wasn't there and had left a message that I should call her. I never did. I worried that I had further damaged Willie's reputation in that Matt would spread the word of my having gone to see his mother. Apparently that didn't happen, much to my relief, because when Will came home the next day, he said that things had gone better, that Matt was nice to him and asked if he was going to be at practice.

Willie also defended Mike who he said has some medical problems. "I think Mike's doctor exam must have affected his thinking. I feel sorry for him," he said. When I asked him how he knew that Mike had medical problems, he said that he had mentioned his problem to Grandma and "she told me that it wasn't anything I was doing but that Mike probably wasn't feeling good, so I asked Matt and he said that Mike had another doctor's appointment." I think it's great that both Willie and Zach feel comfortable with stopping by Mom's room just to talk sometimes.

I can't stand the thought of Willie hurting inside. But I do think he's coping and that he will work things out himself—he's a smart and secure boy. What is the saying—that which doesn't hurt us will make us stronger? All of us have been heaping unsolicited advice on him. His uncles want to beat the stuffing out of Mike (not really) and, short of that, urge Willie to take matters in his own hands. Bill talked to him on the phone and suggested that he can't let kids push him around. We've taught our boys not to start fights and to use fighting only as a last resort to solving problems, but they need to defend themselves—words first, then maybe fists. Anyway, Willie is handling the situation his own way and we're all proud of him. I would suspect that Will's "way" is the same that it's always been—talking. In preschool, he was called "the great compromiser" because he could avoid altercations by convincing his antagonist that the problem wasn't worth fisticuffs. I seem to remember at least one fight he had in elementary school, however, so the verbal method isn't foolproof!

Will and Zach both called friends tonight. You would have thought by the glow on their faces that they talked with the President of the United States. I'm probably $20 poorer, but the happiness they felt at knowing or confirming that their friends hadn't forgotten them was worth the money. Willie showed Pam and Wayne pictures of the party his friends threw for him before we left, and he lovingly talked about each one. He said, "That phone call made me feel a little homesick."

Once again, I felt the guilt stab, but it was fleeting, because deep in my heart I know that the boys are glad they're here, even with their school problems. Just to make sure I'm right, I ask them every once in a while if we should cut our visit short. My suggestion is always quickly shot down. I really believe that bringing them here was the right thing to do, and their lives are being enriched by this experience. I'm hoping that even the school experience will have some redeeming value.

Five

The last days of January and the weather tables have definitely turned. We're having cold, blustery 20-degrees-below-zero weather with lots of new snow. Finally, it appears that we are having a normal full-scale winter.

Yesterday Dad, Roz, Jon and I took Bill (yes, my Bill!) to Thief River where he boarded a plane for Ohio. After a wonderful weekend together, his departure created an immediate void in my life. Let me tell the story.

On Thursday night I met Joyce and Rod in Roseau at 7:00 after picking up the boys from their practices and watching Jenny's basketball game for a while (she was wonderful—played most of the game). We sent the boys home with Gayle and Bill and then proceeded to Thief River where I was led to believe that I was going to accompany Joyce to a meeting with an advisor at Northland College. She ostensibly was going to register for courses in interior decorating and needed me there for moral support. Joyce is very clever; she couldn't have gotten me to Thief River under any other pretense, e.g., shopping. Anyway, when we arrived, Rod said he had to go see a mechanic who sends him a lot of business, and we had half an hour until Joyce's appointment, so he dropped us off at Hardy's. While we were drinking coffee, a familiar voice asked if he could sit down. It was Bill! The shock of recognition was quickly replaced by a shout of pleasure. I was so glad to see him—and truly surprised, thanks to Joyce and Rod who concocted the perfect story for an unsuspecting and trusting victim. They played their parts magnificently and managed to keep the secret from everyone but Dad and Mom who had known of Bill's impending visit for a week.

That night Bill and I slept in Willie's bunk bed while the boys, oblivious to the new development in their lives, slept on at Mom and Dad's. In the morning Mom sent them over to Pam and Wayne's to get ready for school, and we heard them stomping down the stairs at 6:15.

"Hi, Guys!" Bill's greeting caused them to look around for an intercom or something else that projected his voice, and when they saw him in bed they had to touch him to confirm his real presence. The joy on their faces and in their voices was inescapable! We had a big breakfast and Bill took all the kids to school. He and I fooled around all the rest of the day. Joyce came out for lunch and we went over to Gayle's for coffee. That night we took everyone out to eat at the American Legion in Warroad. Chris and Jenny babysat the little kids at separate houses so the task wouldn't be so difficult.

The next day the five of us went snocatting around Bemis Hill and then joined the rest of the family at Tony's hockey game in Baudette. After the game—Roseau won and Tony scored—we met everyone at the Ranch House for something to eat. The service was so slow that Dad, not known for his patience and tolerance for what he considers incompetence, walked out of the restaurant before his food was delivered and feasted on donuts and cider in the magazine section at the drugstore. While everyone was eating and talking at the restaurant, I took the van to the service station and left it there to have a tire patched. I had to walk over the Rainy River Bridge in order to meet my family back at the restaurant, and, even though the walk was less than a mile, the sub-zero temperatures created mascara-blackened tears that streaked my face and blinded my eyes. The state of being cold takes on new meaning when one battles a winter wind in full force over Rainy River! I did thaw out eventually, but my ears and fingers burned for a long time. Bill appreciated my insistence to take the van to the station, leaving him to visit with all of the others. He even said something about "heroic action."

That night Bill and I watched television, played cards (*500*) with Mom and Dad and then *Pictionary* with all of the boys and Pam. It turned out that Chris was convincingly good at the game, and whoever teamed up with him won the round. We also discovered Chris's artistic talents. He drew some amazing pictures! We wouldn't let him quit taking our requests until midnight when we all went to bed.

Sunday found us snocatting in the morning and then piling into the car for Tony's tournament championship game in Baudette and Zach's first hockey game in Warroad. Tony got a ride from Warroad to Baudette, and the rest of us stayed in Warroad to watch Zach play. What a treat that was! The game was exciting with a sudden death overtime that left Roseau the winner with a final score of 2-1. Zach played center with a vengeance! He can't skate as well as most of the other players but his puck handling made up for his skating deficiency. It was easy to understand the soccer influence—he seemed to be fully at home with the passing, dribbling, and shooting. Rod, who had seen him play hockey last winter in Sylvania, commented on the 100% improvement. I really like Zach's coach. He has practices twice a week, plays all of the kids, and seems to keep hockey in perspective, unlike 90% of the people around here.

After the game, Willie had the privilege of watching the Superbowl with his Dad, Chris and the uncles at Rod's party while Joyce, Zach and I picked up Tony in Baudette. I think Willie appreciated the time he could spend with Bill; it made him feel special. When we returned we watched the game for a while, and then I took the boys to the Roseau church for a

Sunday evening youth service where Willie played God in a play about Noah that Pastor Elick had written. It was delightful! Willie's rendition of God was very convincing, and Katie brilliantly starred as Noah's wife. As part of the service, Pastor Elick divided the congregation into three teams for a Bible verse competition. Willie won a point for his team by finding a verse before anyone else; he was the only kid to enjoy that distinction. Zach played hard also. I was proud of both of them.

After the service, Julie Elick told me how much they enjoyed Willie at Released Time classes and what a wonderful person he was. She is also Zach's art teacher at Malung and couldn't say enough nice things about him. To say that I was a proud mother that evening is an understatement! Bill arrived home from the Superbowl party shortly after we returned from church.

On Monday morning Bill took all of the kids to school again where he said goodbye to the boys. I think he was both disappointed and glad that the experience was so untraumatic for them. Will barely acknowledged his departure while Zach remained tearless as he hugged his Dad. I think Bill would like to have seen a little more emotion but the boys, while they were happy to be with their Dad again, were eager to get on with their day. That was good.

After dropping the older kids off at school, Dad, Jon, Roz and I took Bill to Thief River where we had coffee, followed by dinner at the Rex Café and then grocery shopping. We bade him farewell at the airport. Jon and Roz both cried (Roz wanted to go with him in her most melodramatic way) and I felt empty for a while. But we stopped at the library to check out books for Jon and Roz, a book on the North Country for Dad, and *Thornbirds* for me. The visit to the library was the kind of ordinary, routine event that put Bill's visit in perspective: It was a fun, warm surprise soon to become a wonderful memory. I loved him for coming to see us.

The last event of the day was Willie's basketball game at 6:00. Bill felt bad that he had to leave without seeing Willie play, but there was no alternative, and Will said it was no big deal. I was apprehensive based upon a conversation I had had with his coach, who told me that he wouldn't start Willie and probably wouldn't play him much at games because he only went to practice three times a week instead of every day. You can imagine my surprise when Will started, played the whole first quarter, and scored the first two points for his team. He was terrific! He didn't play much after that, which was understandable since there are 18 boys, all of whom played some. Willie was happy, as much for the response from the other boys as for the points. He called his Dad that evening and described the highlights of the game, not all of which, interestingly enough, involved him. He explained in detail several plays made by various members of his team.

And so it goes—another summary of episodes in the lives of the transplanted Patbergs. January is over. Its departure isn't necessarily welcomed because it signals the halfway mark of our Northern Minnesota experience. While riding home after the game, the boys and I discussed the quick passage of time and how abruptly our experience will end. At the end of our discussion, Zach offered this comment: "I can't say that I'll miss anybody at school very much, at least now I can't say that, but I know I'll miss everybody else when I'm gone. It's fun being here." Then Willie added, "But the worst thing about leaving is knowing that we'll never do this again." Sometimes I marvel at the perspicacity of my children!

Six

It's midnight. We just got home from a long day of skiing at Buena Vista. Willie went with the church Youth Group, so Dad, Joyce and I decided to take the rest of the kids also. It was a beautiful sunny day with rising temperatures—perfect for any outdoor activity.

We all had a great time skiing. It was fun watching the little ones zip down the hills with no fear of falling or hitting a tree. There were some minor mishaps, e.g., Jon tripped Auntie Joyce so she plunged face down into the snow and skidded to the bottom of the hill. Everyone was laughing so hard we couldn't ski for a while!

It was hard to get the kids off the slopes at 8:00, but we had to head for home. The Youth Group had a pizza party at the chalet after skiing, and the kids didn't get home on the bus until 1:45 a.m., so Willie stayed with Chris and Jenny at the apartment in town. The rest of us should have been home at 10:00 but we missed the turn going north at Bagley. We drove as far as Shevlin where we stopped to ask for directions, and a sympathetic man led us out of there and on to the right road. We're going to ski at Buena Vista again; five dollars for lift tickets and another five for rentals make the sport affordable.

I skied hard today, almost with the kind of reckless abandonment I felt on the slopes when I was young. It's a fact that I am getting to be more cautious as I age—no more sky diving, wild roller coasters, fast skiing. All of my Peace Corps adventures are wistful memories. I'm afraid to take risks anymore. Is it because I have children and am responsible for someone other than myself? I miss the old excitement.

Another wonderful weekend with weather made to order! The kids had four days with no school, and they played most of the time—no practices, no school work, only a little piano, lots of snocatting, and visits to the hunting shack where Gayle and Bill were staying.

On Saturday Dad, Mom, the boys and I went on a long, scenic snocat ride east of the Conner Bridge and back of Bemis Hill. The boys did some sledding at the Hill where we had cookies and cocoa afterward. Willie and Zach drove the snocats, Willie skillfully cautious and Zach more recklessly. Jonathan fell asleep on my snocat, snuggled between me and Lucy who was somewhat tentative about the whole experience, this being her first time riding open air on a fast machine. When we returned home, the boys practiced the piano a little and then all of us snocatted up to the shack to visit Gayle and Bill.

We went to church on Sunday and found Joyce, Sharon and Jena waiting for us when we returned. Mom and I babysat Jena and Hannah while Joyce, Katie and Jon (on the Panther), Dad and Zach (Jag 1), Pam and Roslyn (the Lynx) and Sharon and Linsay (Jag 2) snocatted to Dewey's to pick up some treats and the Sunday paper. It was the kind of day you'd like to bottle up and save for inclement weather. Temperatures in the 30s melted icicles hanging from the eaves and transformed the landscape into a sea of shimmering gold. Katie waxed poetic when she described how the bright blue sky provided a breath-taking contrast with the snow-clad, dark green evergreens that formed a canopy over the narrow trails (well, she didn't use those words, but her images were just as vivid!). Jonathan, lulled to sleep as usual by the sound of the noisy motors and the roller-coaster movement, told Mom later that he dreamt about "nice monsters" while snuggled between Katie and Joyce. He became perturbed when he was interrupted by Roz who said, "Me too, Jon, I dreamt about nice monsters."

Jon replied, "No, you didn't, Rozie, you're just saying that. Grandma, isn't Rozie just saying that?!" Everyone expressed regret that the two-hour expedition had to end.

Meanwhile, Chris and Willie were discovering new uses for the snocat on that bright afternoon. At one point they drove at full speed into the grove on the Cheetah, pulling Jenny on a makeshift sled. They paused only long enough to ask Wayne for some tape to keep the rope on the sled from slipping while they roared around the yard. When they got tired of that game, they took a break and watched a little TV with Tony (who was sick), Mom and me. Mom made them sandwiches and a thermos of cocoa, which they took with them to the hunting shack, where they spent the rest of the afternoon ski-boarding down the snowdrifts on the side of the cow pond.

I had a nice time talking with Mom and befriending Jena who never once uttered her traditional trademark wail, "Judy, NOOOOOOOOO!" We visited the rabbit, which she immediately identified as a bunny, and I pulled her around the yard in her custom made sled. She was the picture of wonderfulness—plump face firmly encased in a pink hood attached to a jacket that matched the smallest pair of pink boots I'd ever seen. She wore a long denim dress over pink tights covered by green sweat pants—an odd combination of clothes by Vogue standards but very appealing on Jena. She responded positively to Mom's suggestion that Uncle Wayne take her to see the cows, but when the time came for him to pick her up, she howled vociferously and rejected his advances, as usual. This time, however, Wayne just took her and she stopped crying ten feet from the house. When he brought her back, she kept asking, "Where Wayne?" and "See cows?" Her response delighted Mom and me because, up until now, Jena has never wanted anything to do with Wayne (or any man). He calls her "Truck."

That evening we all climbed on the snocats again (we have four now that I bought one) to pay Gayle and Bill one last visit at the shack before they returned to civilization. Weekends at the hunting cabin have been booked for the duration of the winter; everyone wants to stay up there. I know we want to get one more weekend in before we leave.

The weekend was not without disappointment, however. Pam told me that her new babysitter won't let me take care of Hannah, not even one day a week. I can hardly bear the thought of not attending to the needs of that sweet little person any time during the week. She's become such a natural part of my routine and I'll miss her a lot.

I have a strong feeling that my biggest regret one day will be that I was not a good mother to my sons, and I won't have a chance to rectify my parenting mistakes. I'm already tormented by questions: Am I loving them enough? Will I someday be able to forget the horrible breakdowns of love that I know will take place when I fail to control my unfocused anger and take it out on my innocent children who can't fight back? Will I find myself remembering those moments and forgetting the wonderful times when I was so good in my mother role, when I communicated to my sons the adoration for them that I feel from the depths of my being? Will they be able to forgive me someday? I hope I won't cause my sons too much pain when they are older. I hope I'm not causing them pain now.

I find myself thinking a lot about missed opportunities that haven't happened yet—things that I will unknowingly not do that have the potential of making my children happier, more compassionate people. Is that not strange thinking, I wonder?

Mom is retiring next year after thirty years of teaching all elementary grades, but mostly first and second. She has decided that it's time to relinquish her position to a younger person. This decision instills in all those who know her the mixed feelings of congratulatory support, because she deserves an easier life, and infinite sadness because she is, simply, the best teacher. She has had a positive influence on hundreds of students, many of whom still live in this community. I know this to be true because I hear it from people of all ages. So do my brother and sisters who have lived in this area all of their lives. From the brightest, we hear comments to the effect that she inspired them to do great things, and from the less intellectually endowed, the remarks touch on her patience when success didn't come easily for them.

In my mother's mind, every child can succeed; each one has his own potential in some area of expertise. I don't know how many times I've heard her say during conversations about a child who isn't doing well academically, "But you should see him work with his hands . . . ." or "Give her a little more time and she'll catch up." She always tries to give these children as much time as they need in order to learn, even when her own time is at a premium because she has to meet the needs of so many other children. I have never heard my mother speak negatively or disparagingly about a child.

The research on teacher effectiveness has failed to produce incontrovertible data on the qualities that make an effective teacher. Is the ideal teacher warm or reserved? Is she strict or lenient? Is she rigorous or flexible? Does she speak loudly or softly? Is he a friend to the children, or does he insist on maintaining strict teacher-student roles? Is he a nurturing kind of person or one who feels his time is better spent in teaching the subject matter? Does he treat all of his students equally, or does he judiciously discriminate in the giving of his time? All of these questions, and many others, are continually researched in order to draw a profile of an effective teacher. The time spent on this task is, I think, wasted because the best teacher, e.g., my mother, is all of the above at various times and in different circumstances.

At the present time, Mom is teaching seven second graders and ten first graders. I don't think she's ever had a single grade classroom, which she thinks would be a luxury for her but not necessarily ideal for the children. Teaching two grades requires twice as much of everything necessary to keep the classroom running smoothly—monitoring, patience, preparation, organization and energy. But Mom believes that her children have never been short-changed, and that the benefits of a two-grade classroom—fostering independence, encouraging cooperative learning, accepting responsibility, practicing controlled restraint and learning patience—outweigh the negatives, which undeniably include less teacher time for individual students. At a recent PTO meeting, a heated discussion arose over a proposal for single-grade classrooms in Malung and Wannaska, with the two schools dividing the country population so that one school would house the first three grades, and the other would house grades four through six. This arrangement would make life easier for the teachers but wreak havoc in the lives of families whose children could be divided among three schools (including high school in Roseau). The teachers voiced opinions in favor of a proposal that actually presented the children as victims in an inferior learning situation. Mom thinks that they were using the children as disguises for their real concern which focuses on themselves. It's not that she's against change in principle—only in situations such as this one, where the change is no better or creates more problems than the status quo.

I've observed Mom's teaching many times and, as a fellow educator, I think she's great. I think I'm impressed with her gentleness and patience most of all. She has received countless love letters from her children over the years, e.g., "I love you so much, Mrs. Pearson." She despises labels that stigmatize kids and would rather mainstream handicapped children then have them go to special classes where they learn to be different. She doesn't need a battery of tests to inform her that a child has an attention deficit or hasn't fully developed fine motor coordination. She knows these things because the child has trouble attending to a task or can't form his letters well. She treats the symptoms just as if they'd been formally diagnosed in a testing situation. One day I watched while she very subtly and skillfully used a child's strengths to help him with his weaknesses. I couldn't hear the conversation, but I could tell by the look on his face that he was happy—perhaps because Mom made his problems seem a little less insurmountable. It's so sad that when a powerful, effective, wonderful teacher retires, all of her knowledge retires with her.

I did nothing scholarly or literary today and I didn't feel guilty! My daily struggle to justify my sabbatical is, I think, subsiding, if not completely over. Today I feel at total peace with myself and with my existence. Dad and I walked three miles this morning and I made dinner for him and Wayne, as usual. But yesterday and today I prepared the meal without giving any thought to the work I thought I should be doing. After dinner, I read the newspapers and listened while Dad told Roz and Jon the story of *Peter Rabbit* (one of four stories in his repertoire, the others being *Tumiliten, The Boy and the Dike,* and *Nail Soup*—the same ones he told me while I was growing up). Then I lay down with the kids and read them a story until they fell asleep. While they were napping, I did the dishes at Mom's and Pam's but never finished at Pam's because Dad called to see if I wanted to go snocatting. We took Roz and Jon sledding at Bemis Hill on the snocats and arrived home just in time to greet Pam and the school bus. After a snack Zach and I took a snocat ride around the town line. He drove and I hugged him tightly. I made pancakes and bacon for supper and spent the rest of the evening babysitting sweet Hannah while Pam took the kids to Youth Group and Adventure Club. A boring day, you say? Not a bit: It was the kind of day everyone should have. I had fun, was useful, and spent time just letting my thoughts wander. Mom remarked on how nice it is to have me around and how much I'll be missed when I leave. Dad and Wayne appreciate my cooking. It feels good to be needed.

Pam and I managed to get a walk in before she left with the kids. Despite our age difference, we feel the same way about a lot of things, especially those that involve our children, and our walks are never long enough to exhaust conversation topics. Pam was, and still is, a young mother. She had her fourth child at the same age I had my first. Of course, I was well on my way to middle age when I entered motherhood! One of the things we talked about today is whether it is better for married couples to have their children when they are young and then have a lot of time to play after the children are grown (Pam and Wayne), or if most of the playing should occur before children, which leaves less time for play after they're grown (Bill and I). I guess the jury is still out for both of us. Pam is tough and smart with an inimitable laugh. She brings a kind of levity to a family that has a tendency to be too serious sometimes.

What is the mysterious glue that holds my family together? Is it a complex chemistry? Is it the affection that intertwines us? Is it the strong family ties that can ultimately set all things right, or the bond we share that makes us forget the contentious times? Is it the story of how we care for each other? I suspect that it's all of these, plus the need to ignore the bad things sometimes in order to all get along.

During my first year of teaching in Connecticut, I had a friend who wrote me letters from a Minnesota prison where he was incarcerated for armed robbery. His letters had a profound effect on my teaching. He was fascinating in his ability to stimulate even the laziest mind (mine) to think about important things, such as writing. I remember thinking that my friend was an intellectual giant of sorts who just couldn't encapsulate his enormous brain power to further the cause of mankind in any productive way. This incapability on his part was nothing short of sinful in my own mind, since I wanted more than anything else at that time in my life to be considered an intellectual. So when my friend committed his crime and was sent to prison, I wasn't surprised in the least; in fact, I was more convinced than ever that he was just too intelligent for society's norms, and I even romanticized his fate—really, it was the only appropriate course of action someone as intelligent as my friend could be forced into taking.

I was flattered to think that my friend thought me intellectually worthy enough to be the recipient of his letters, and I read them many times. I also composed letters to him but sent only those that I deemed sophisticated enough for him. One of the lessons I learned from him that I imparted to my 7th grade students had to do with writing. He was adamant that I should encourage them to write, feeling strongly as he did, I suspect, because his teachers never encouraged him to write. He warned me not to give them a little packet of what he called "stifling ideas," such as mother, God, country, and summer vacation, but rather let them select one plain, simple material object—a chair, a book, tree, clock, anything concrete—and let them say what they wanted to say. Now, those were the days of the theme, well-formed paragraphs, grammatical correctness, red-inked rough drafts and trite topics that were the same for everyone. My friend told me that I had a beautiful opportunity to really help kids write for the purpose of wanting to say something.

At the same time he was giving me advice, my friend was writing the great American novel, which he believed wouldn't be discovered until he was dead because no one would publish it. Nevertheless, he was taking a couple of correspondence courses on writing (along with Spanish and Russian) from the University of Minnesota and had submitted 16,000 words of his book to a professor, who fired back such a positive reaction that my friend was convinced of his ability to publish. Talk about empowerment!

I remember that my friend articulated thoughts such as "A soul is kind of a tender thing, like a person with no skin" and "Thinking is like a river flowing by and all you have by way of equipment to pick a little of it out is a cup, or maybe even a bucket . . . . Look at all you miss by having the handicap of just being able to use puny words—spoken or on paper—to capture some of the thoughts and feelings . . . . A cup is even too big in the analogy . . . ."

In one of the last letters I received from him, he thanked me for the Easter card I had sent and for my prayers and for thinking about him in my loneliness ("my" loneliness, not his). He went on to say that he didn't know if he was practiced enough in praying to return my prayers, but he wanted me to know that he was thinking of me and wishing that he were a poet instead of a scribbler in prose. He said that if the right wishes were gold, I would surely be a queen, but if I kept on being myself, I wouldn't even need the crown. I doubt that I appreciated those sentiments but, to a lonely transplanted beginning teacher, they gave me a lot of comfort. My friend ended that letter by inviting me to write when I could but only when I felt like it. He did not want me to feel that I owed it to him to write.

Mary Ann called the other day to ask about Boyne skiing plans. She told me that Bill is very lonesome and is secretly hoping that we will go home from Boyne. I felt terrible and actually thought about going home early but I know I can't—we're not ready to leave. I cannot express often enough my gratitude to

Bill for letting me have this experience; most husbands would not have permitted the abandonment.

Even though it's a cliché, it's also a powerful revelation, especially when you're in your 50s and 60s (I know from talking to women who are there): Everyone says that time goes by so fast that you're desperate to savor and remember every moment. I'm already feeling that pressure in my 40s and I know it's going to get worse. There's a scientific explanation for that phenomenon that has to do with how many years you've lived and how many you have left. I can't remember the formula.

I already wish that I could hold back time—keep my children with me, young and innocent. I remember the boys when they were babies with such sweetness my heart aches. I love them fiercely. I'm absolutely enchanted by their personalities. They are so different, with special attributes that I recognize and must nurture to help them grow in faith and love. I worry that I don't always hear them. I listen, but do I really hear? When they grow up, I want them to have a glorious sense of independence. I want them to do good things in the world.

The boys bring out the best in Bill and me, and we act more lovingly together when we're with them than when we're alone.

I see the essence of my sons, but what they become will be a surprise. I hope I don't become unhinged when they leave me.

Seven

Another beautiful winter day. Willie is going skiing at Buena Vista again, this time with his sixth grade class. He's excited, especially since he's going with a friend whom he also invited to go on the 4H ski trip in a couple of weeks. Mom said that he looks happy at school—talking and laughing with kids. She said that the boys stop by her room to say, "Hi, Grandma" every day. I think they just like knowing she's there.

I asked Zach if kids are beating up on him in school and he replied, "Not much." I laughed because he's so phlegmatic about his rough treatment. The other day Dad asked him about Mike and Zach said, "Well, he pushed me against the boards again today so I pushed him back. This time he moved a little. But, Grandpa, you should have seen Tony and me fight him at the last recess—boy, we got him good!"

The boys' report cards were fine—Zach with a lot of "Excellents" and "Satisfactory Plusses" and Willie with a B average. They don't work very hard, especially Zach who has no homework at all. They also received high marks on piano lessons.

This absolutely perfect weather makes me euphoric! I'm sitting on the sofa in front of the window basking in the sunshine and watching Rozie and Jonathan frolic in the snow with the three dogs. The only unhappy customers in this scenario are the birds, whose efforts to get to the feeder are hampered by the children's play. After dinner, which Dad is preparing (a Swedish meat, potato, and onion soup dish called *Lopskas*), we'll take the kids for a snocat ride. They'll have to take a nap and then Aunt Myrtle and Uncle Raymond are bringing Jody over to play. This evening I'll pick up Willie at the high school and Zach at the hockey rink.

Dad, Wayne, and I had a discussion about religion this morning. We all agreed that fundamentalist (charismatic?) Christians have reaped more harm than good in this world, and many continue to give Christianity a bad name. The latest example is Jimmy Swaggert, a popular televangelist who admitted to having sexual trysts with prostitutes. It makes me furious to think about the millions of people who have supported his ministry, even when they couldn't afford to, and now feel betrayed by his anti-Christian behavior. At the same time, I feel that Swaggert shouldn't necessarily be held to a higher standard than the rest of us because he too is an imperfect human being, as vulnerable to sin as the rest of us. So, if one believed in his message before the fall, there should be no reason to change direction. I think it's his self-righteous smugness—the audacious conviction that he has it right and those who don't agree with him have it wrong—that prevents me from wishing him well. If Jimmy Swaggert, and rest of his ilk, would exhibit just a modicum of uncertainty about their Christian faith—admit that God is a mystery and, as such, we don't have all of the answers—I would be inclined to listen more and criticize less. Dad didn't buy into my analysis one hundred percent, but he thinks I'm on the right track.

Closer to home, we have situations in our small churches that confirm what agnostics and atheists have posited about organized religion for a long time: Jesus Christ is noticeably absent in the way we live. Most fundamentalist Christians are conservative Republicans who can't extol Ronald Reagan's virtues enough. As such, they possess a deep-seated, irrational fear of Communism and the Soviet Union. One is looked at suspiciously if he happens to even suggest a positive aspect of the system. He's anti-Christian if he posits a pro-choice position. There are no gradations of right and wrong; everything is pretty much black and white. It's always been a mystery to me why more churchgoers aren't Democrats, since the politics of the Democratic Party are far more compatible with Christianity than are those of the Republicans. After all, Jesus Christ helped the poor, the disenfranchised, and the helpless. Shouldn't Christians do likewise? Doesn't the Democratic Party reflect this value by implementing and supporting programs that help people who cannot do it all themselves? It's the abortion issue that makes many people vote Republican, I know that. But abortion shouldn't be a political issue when it comes to voting, because neither party does much about the problem when it's in office. People ask me how I can vote Democratic when to do so is casting a vote for abortion. I try to explain that the majority of Democrats are not in favor of abortion; they're against the government telling them how to run our lives.

Why do so many Christians seem to be inhumane in their outlook on life? They actually say things such as "people in America are poor because they want to be and any kind of government assistance makes them lazier and more dependent." They don't change expressions when they're reminded that rats bite babies in the slums of big cities, or that Appalachian children live in shacks with dirt floors. Many skirt any kind of responsibility for helping those who are less fortunate than they. Indeed, they believe that the poor are less fortunate because they don't work hard enough.

So many Christians are as ignorant about homelessness as they are about poverty. The homeless are in the streets because they want to be there. Never mind that their leader, George Bush himself, acknowledged that only about 30% of the homeless have mental problems, which result in a choice to live on the streets, and the rest are there because of unfortunate circumstances. I've heard people say that no one needs to live on the streets in America. Whatever happened to compassion?

I am a Christian. I'm also liberal in my political views, determined to keep an open mind, and free of racial prejudice as far as I can tell. I believe that the poor will always be marginalized, on this earth anyway. I feel sorry for people who try but just can't break the poverty cycle. My heart goes out to the homeless, and I'm accepting of other people's lifestyles. I fear pollution more than communism and believe in public education for all its ills. I believe that God made a beautiful world which man has ruined, so now we all have a responsibility to help each other while here on earth—no exceptions. I'm raising my sons to be compassionate and to feel responsible for those less fortunate than they.

I believe that God intervenes in our lives today in ways we can't understand. I believe in life after death and Jesus as the one who can provide the best life here on earth and in Heaven. I enjoy dialoguing with people holding viewpoints different from my own, but I get impatient when they won't change their minds. I love people of all races and religions, including fundamentalist Christians. I wish I were a more effective defender of my faith, but I'm beginning to conclude that those who don't believe will find no explanation of mine acceptable anyway. I still wish I could be more articulate when the opportunity to defend my faith arises.

I absolutely believe that God created the world, and I think that belief is compatible with scientific theories of evolution. The randomness and chance aspects of evolution bother me a little, but I believe that God was, and still is, is in control of that process also. If God wanted "chance" to create His universe, that's okay with me. I also have a little problem with the evolution of human beings but, there, again, God was in control of whatever He wanted our origins to be. Our soul comes from God and that's what's important. When I think about death, which can happen at any time, and life, which is a gift, I don't know how anyone cannot believe in God. To do that is to assert that there is nothing beyond this life. And that's depressing.

I believe that the world is full of beautiful people, and if we respond to them as Christ responded to people, they will show us the face of Christ (Calvin); that love, once it's destroyed or damaged cannot be made whole again, so we need to watch out how we treat love; that all of my good ideas come from better thinkers before me and their ideas have now become mine—they're all mixed up; that tolerance is not a nice word because we shouldn't just put up with people who have ideas different from ours but rather accept and embrace them (the people, not the ideas); that it's a wonderful thing to be young—the young have an elation that gets lost with age; that if you do what's in your heart, you'll be fine; that trees and quilts are wonderful legacies because they provide beauty, comfort, solace and warmth, and they're both acts of love; that we must have a sense of how much better we can be at any age; that the greatest gift God gave us is free will, although I'm not sure it's always a gift, and I don't think it is the whole answer to why there is suffering in the world; that we all think we deserve so much better than what we have or if we have a lot, we justify our good fortune by reminding ourselves how hard we've had to work to get where we are.

The Big Bang Theory—is it really the only theory that can sufficiently explain our existence? I've heard that, and I don't believe it. The world came into existence in an instant. What existed before the Big Bang? Where did the energy that exploded come from? Science can't explain everything.

I don't think that science even has the potential to explain everything, and it isn't just the case that we haven't found all of the paradigms yet.

I inherited my Christian faith and values, but I have chosen to uphold and nurture them. If one's faith depends on inheritance only, then it will eventually shrivel and die.

Eight

We awoke to the sound of the wind blowing new-fallen snow. The trees are once again clad in white and the world smells fresh.

During our snocat ride yesterday, we followed tracks belonging to a pack of timber wolves. I was so excited, thinking that at any moment we would encounter those primitive, rare, and very special animals, but they eluded us. Then last night, Dad called to tell me that if I wanted to hear sounds of the wild I should step outside. I did and heard nothing. I waited about five minutes on Wayne's deck and then I heard them—the wolves. My senses were keen—every nerve taut—and, as I listened to the howling, I turned back the clock thirty years to a time when timber wolves were so prevalent that one was struck by the stillness of the night when they were silent. I remember as a child waking up at midnight and stumbling downstairs to find my mother mopping the kitchen floor and holding herself, not because she was cold, but because the wolves were so close to the house. The howling chilled her bones. She said it sounded like lost babies calling their mother. But even while the thin wails were chilling, they were also mesmerizing, and we were drawn to them like a mother driven to find her lost child.

Last night was the first time I had heard the wolves since I left home and my response hadn't changed. I was still both chilled and mesmerized. I also felt tremendously relieved and happy to know that the wolves are still here, reminding us that the wild continue to live in this tame land.

Pam told me the story of how she and Wayne rescued a baby timber wolf last spring. It had apparently strayed from the den and had been trampled by cows in the pasture. They wrapped him up in a coat and took him to the side of the woods south of the house where they stayed with him for three hours until he started to walk. When they checked up on him the next day, he was gone. They hoped that his mother had found him.

We went to Grand Forks to see my cousin who is at the Rehabilitation Center there recovering from a major illness that required a shunt to be implanted in his brain. He has been deprived of the ability to walk, talk, and swallow. This was our second visit. Our first visit a month ago was achingly depressing. My cousin could understand everything that was going on and knew us but could do nothing to communicate or express himself. I felt, at the same time, a deep sadness accompanying my focused anger and an intense gratitude for my health and the health of my children. My cousin cried silently when I asked him about his kids, and I stirred up nostalgia for everything normal and familiar—family, home, work, play, drinking coffee around the kitchen table. I thought about how easily we take things for granted and how blessed we truly are.

Today I approached our return visit with dread, having heard conflicting reports about his progress. Imagine my joy when my cousin greeted me with a smile, "Hi, Judy," and took another sip of coffee. He spoke haltingly and infrequently, taking several seconds to process a question at times, but he could communicate. Nostalgia still swept over him whenever we reminisced or speculated about the future—sometimes unleashing a stream of tears—but he looked comparatively good. His hair had even grown back a little. His wife has found an apartment in East Grand Forks where they both will be living in a couple of weeks.

We met Grandma Rosie who was returning from a visit with her relatives in North Dakota and had been dropped off at the Rehabilitation Center. Our ride home was pleasantly enhanced by her presence. I always take the opportunity to probe Grandma for information about the past and she willingly complies. She sang old songs and humored Jonathan when he became restless. I do love and admire her so much! She's 86 years old and just as assertive and spirited as ever. Physically, she's slowing down a bit—no spring in her step anymore—but mentally she's as sharp as ever. She travels as much as she can in order to visit her eleven children—plane (granddaughter's wedding in New Jersey with a side trip to New York City), train, and chauffeured car—even hitching rides with relatives and friends who are going her way.

One of the nicest aspects of the day was spending time with Mom who, because of her job, never accompanies Dad and me on our excursions. I enjoyed her company tremendously.

That night we went to a Valentine party at the Roseau Covenant Church, which featured a homemade version of "The Newlywed Game"—created, organized and supervised by none other than my sister Gayle. She wrote all of the questions—not an easy task, I suspect—and I'm impressed by her cleverness. I arrived late because we didn't get back from Grand Forks until 7:15, so I missed dinner and the "leg game." I heard that Pam guessed the owner of a fine pair of male legs but couldn't identify her husband's! It was a hilarious night.

For some reason—maybe it was the church event—I've been thinking a lot about my struggle with faith these days. Growing up, I went regularly to church and Sunday School, as did most of the people in my small town. It was a moralistic church with a kind of thou-shalt-not approach, but I learned about God, Jesus, and the Bible and, for that body of knowledge, I'm grateful. There was also a lot of love and concern in my church and so I felt good when I went, as if I knew that church was where I belonged and that being there was right.

I didn't want to go every Sunday, especially after a late Saturday night, but I never argued or rebelled out of respect for my parents (at least that's the way I remember it!). I recall thinking at the time that if there were more emphasis on God's love and less on the dangers of Hell, I probably wouldn't feel the pressure to live such a nervously clean life. Because of the pulpit rhetoric—sometimes fiery—I was afraid to go to sleep at night unless I had prayed that God would forgive my sins and take me to Heaven if I died. I worried that God would come for me when I was doing something that He wouldn't approve of, such as dancing. But those fear moments were few and far between. I have to say that I was a "good" Christian during high school and did very few things that I felt would have negative spiritual consequences. All in all, it was a carefree and happy time in my life.

In college I tried to break out of this "goodness" mold with varying degrees of success. I went to parties with my boyfriend and best friend and occasionally drank, something I never even tried in high school. I went to church infrequently and tried not to think about all the rules I was breaking. My goal was to act out my beliefs without sacrificing too much fun. I guess the prevailing philosophy in my life during those years was that Christians couldn't have a lot of fun—so I just hoped (and prayed) that I could delay or prevent anything bad from happening to me until I was older and ready to live a truly good Christian life. Through it all, though, I never lost my faith. The fundamentals of Christianity—spelled out in the Apostles Creed—never left my heart.

The times I went to church in college because I wanted to were good for me spiritually. I remember going to a revival meeting in Bemidji with my parents when they came to visit. Nicky Cruz, a former drug addict in New York City who was rescued by Dave Wilkerson of Teen Challenge, was the speaker and he spoke to me that night. I remember feeling a strong desire to have a closer relationship with Christ—I wanted to be good, to be authentic—but I could not make the commitment. Did I feel guilty? Yes, but what I felt most anxious about, even more than the guilt and condemnation, was death and my fate. And then there were the times when I felt most anxious about life itself. Is there any meaning to life? What are people for? Why did God create us? Why does He allow evil in the world? I kept asking the hard questions, and there were people in my life who tried to answer them, but they failed to assure me that it was okay to ask those questions in the first place. In fact, I was led to believe that entertaining such questions bordered on doubting my faith, and doubting was definitely wrong. I was told over and over again that God was a mystery, and I needed to wait until I got to Heaven where He would answer all my questions.

Teaching in an economically deprived school in Connecticut allowed (forced?) me to act on my faith, to put my compassion to work in helping my students with their lives. I started reading the Bible and going to church regularly again—a more liberal, non-denominational church. I was desperate to be a good Christian, to reach out to people who needed help. My friends were non-believers who didn't give much thought to spiritual things. I tried to understand how they could go through life without faith in God, something that was so important to me, even during the times my faith waned. And it did. My determination to live closer to God waxed and waned—I just couldn't make the total forever commitment.

It was my two years in the Peace Corps, and the months of traveling afterwards, that forced me back to the "old-time religion" of my growing up years (the good parts). I felt so far removed from anything familiar that I reached for and held tightly to my faith. I was grateful for the Bible verses I had memorized in Sunday School and recited them whenever I felt lonely, afraid, or physically threatened which was quite often. I guess you could say that I returned to my faith roots out of a need for God, to know that He was in control of my life at a time when I couldn't be. I prayed all of the time; Psalm 23 was my prayer of choice. I never stopped praying the time I had to go to the Peace Corps office in Manila during a particularly hard monsoon season, and the streets were under water, inhabited by cobras which had slithered down from the mountains. I never stopped praying when I got altitude sickness and was scared that I would die of pulmonary edema on my way to the base camp at Mount Everest. When the guy I was trekking with placed a bag over my head to help me breathe and took me down the mountain a couple of hundred feet, I knew that God was in control, and I would live. I never stopped praying on my way back to Kathmandu when I had to inch my way across a slippery rock leading into a raging river, numb with the fear that I was going to die. I had reached the halfway mark when I slipped on the rock and lost my grip. As I was plunging toward the frothy water, something made me reach out and grasp a branch, the only one hanging over the rock. That move saved my life. I knew that Divine Intervention had once again saved me. This conviction was confirmed when, in reading a letter from my mother a week later, she asked me if I had been in trouble on the exact day that I was plunging toward the river. She said in her letter that she had prayed throughout that night that God would save me from whatever danger I was in.

These are just three incidences where God saved me from death or injury; there were other times during my Peace Corps experience when I found myself in trouble. Because of my need for Him, it was relatively easy to be the good Christian that I had strived to be all the years before.

During four years of graduate school at the University of Minnesota, I went to church fairly regularly but was overcome with spiritual ennui, except for the times I went home to the farm. I had met Bill, who would later become my husband, in Thailand and was waiting for him to get out of the Peace Corps, so my social life for the first year was pretty tame. Bill joined me, and over the next three years it became increasingly clear that we were going to be married. I knew I loved Bill and thought at the time that his non-believer status didn't matter very much. I was worried about our future children, but Bill assured me that he would not oppose my taking them to church and making sure they had a religious foundation, just as he had growing up. He believed that this foundation was important so they could responsibly make their own decisions someday. He remains true to his word and supports me in our sons' religious training.

My attention to God became undivided the day my oldest son was born. I was so grateful to God for Willie that I promised Him I would raise this child, and any others He would bless me with, to love and obey Him. And I'm keeping this promise, as best I can. I am determined to do everything in my power to equip my sons with a strong faith, something I feel they need badly in order to survive (thrive) in this world. I am particularly zealous in light of the fact that my sons are growing up with only one parent who is a Christian and another who is a wonderful father but not a believer. Once in a while the boys ask why their Dad doesn't go to church, but they seem to be surprisingly okay with the situation as it exists. They have asked me if Daddy will go to Heaven when he dies, and I assure them that God will take care of their father. For now, they seem to be satisfied with that simple answer. I don't know what I'll say when their questions become harder to answer, as they most likely will. I do know that I will continue to try to make their faith foundation so strong that it will sustain them when they become older. I can't do that without my church. One of the reasons I need my church is so

I can have contemporary support for the traditional values that I believe are so important in raising my children.

I am grateful for my relationship with God over the years. Even during the rockiest of times, I never lost my faith. My spiritual future is unpredictable—I don't know where God will take me—but I know He has a plan for the rest of my life.

Nine

February 11th and another family gathering at the hunting cabin—the occasion this time was Joyce's birthday. Everyone, except Pam and Hannah (Hannah is not feeling well), snocatted up to the cabin where we had the supper Joyce had made and a cake I had baked. Freddy and Bev were there. So were Dale and Shawn who was in top form. Every family occasion graced by Shawn's presence is marked by a lot of laughter, because she is so funny.

Dad and I ended up walking the mile because, even though we have a combined total of five snocats, there weren't enough to go around! During our walk, Dad commented on the crazy side of our family. Getting together for everybody's birthday, whether the person is nine or ninety, in all kinds of weather and under inconvenient circumstances, qualifies as an example of our craziness, I guess. In spite of our vast differences in personalities and ages, it goes without saying that all of us will choose family events over other activities most of the time. Zach, for example, missed his hockey game because Joyce and Rod invited him and Tony to stay overnight and go ice fishing. As enamored with hockey as he is, Zach still decided he'd rather be with them than play. In a world constant only in its flux, the continuity of birthday parties and other family events is comforting.

Willie missed his basketball game at Malung on Saturday also. Joyce took him to the game only to have to go home because he had forgotten his uniform, which Willie thought was in his bag. He was disappointed but not crushed.

Another weekend slips into the past, never to be lived again. Time is passing quickly. No matter how much we try to savor the moments, they don't linger so we have to settle for a lot of tastes. Hopefully, our memories of our sojourn here won't just consist of general feelings of a "good time" but separate meaningful incidents that we don't want to forget.

I'm sitting in Hardy's waiting for Zach to finish hockey practice. I have to pick up Jon and Roz at Grandma Rosie's in a few minutes. They couldn't go to story hour at the library this morning because Gayle is out of town, but they wanted to visit Grandma so they could give her the Valentines they had made for her.

Those two little people bring more joy into my life than I could ever have imagined. As my constant companions, I feel a definite void when they're not around. They have very different personalities so they squabble a lot, but something holds them tightly together. Roz is the undisputed leader who feels that her calling in life is to keep Jon in line. "Go give Grandpa a kiss and a hug now, Jon," she orders. Jonathan dutifully obeys. Every once in a while he beats her to the punch though, and she falls apart. A fight ensues and we have a cacophonous assault on our ears—Jon wailing for Daddy and Roz for Mommy (or Grandma if her mother is around).

It is 9 a.m. and we are on our way to Michigan for our annual family ski trip at Boyne. For the past several years the Patbergs and friends from Toledo and the Minnesota gang have gotten together for skiing at Boyne over Presidents' weekend. This year would be no exception, even though there is only one Patberg left in Toledo. Our plan this year is to meet Bill at the houses we rented. We have been on the road battling a fierce blizzard since 7:00 last night (14 hours!). All of us are bone weary, so tired that sleep eludes us when we close our eyes. Our tension is relieved only by the hope that we'll be skiing in lots of fresh powder tomorrow. The worst scenario has us arriving at Boyne to find that it hasn't snowed there so skiing conditions are mediocre at best. After this nightmarish trip, that discovery would be a terrible injustice.

School was cancelled at Malung yesterday and today because water pipes burst at the high school. So, in the midst of packing for our ski trip I had to make dinner for all the kids. On Wednesday night I stayed up until 2 a.m. making lasagne to take with us, so I really needed to take a nap yesterday but it never materialized.

When we stopped at a gas station an hour ago, I called Bill to see how his plans were shaping up. He said that he had finally made it home after being snowbound in Chicago where he had driven for a business trip. He sounded cheerful—why shouldn't he, having to travel only five hours today under drivable conditions!

After driving 21 hours in blizzard conditions we arrived at the Boyne house at 4:30 p.m. to find Bill and Tom and Matthew Stibbe—and a roaring fire—waiting for us. Skiing was superb—lots of snow and relatively mild weather. By the third day, Jonathan was skiing with us down everything but the expert mogul runs. He loved the attention and the feeling of accomplishment. But thinking about Rozie humbled him, as usual. "Yah, when I tell Rozie that I can ski good now—can stop, turn right, turn left, and I skied Camelot, Kathy's Run, Amy's Run, McGully, Long John's, she'll just say, 'Oh, I can do that too' and wiggle her hips and walk away!" We laughed so hard our sides hurt, especially since we knew that he was right. It turned out to be almost exactly what Rozie said. Jon loved being with Bill.

I caught glimpses of the bigger kids tearing up the slopes and gobbling down sandwiches, but most of the time they remained out of sight. Very excited to see Bill initially, Will and Zach's enthusiasm for being with their father was soon replaced by their passion for fast skiing, something their father can appreciate but not share. I shudder when I picture Zach and Tony sailing off the ledge, over our heads, and landing a few feet from where we were standing, our faces frozen in anticipation of the snow shower that we knew would cover us from head to foot. And then there are the images of Willie, Chris, and Matt careening through the woods, missing trees by inches, waving and yelling to those of us who are traversing down the hill. The girls were not far behind, but they always appeared to be in much more control of their situation than the boys! For both sexes, the missing ingredient was fear—or so it seemed. Maybe they were scared. All I know is that in both scenarios, the perpetrators committed their crimes amid peals of laughter, which we translated as a kind of mockery for our safe skiing.

And how did I fare with Bill? Not so well, actually. This was once again a situation where expectations and anticipation were far greater than the actual event. Despite our best efforts, Bill and I were mad at each other much of the time. I just don't understand how two people can be so excited at the prospect of seeing each other only to react so differently when they're finally together! We succeeded in being friendly during the day while we were skiing and had fun, but at night there was little intimacy—only hard feelings. I found myself sleeping next to Bill, wondering what he was thinking and afraid to ask him. Is it possible that the chasm has gotten too wide to ever be bridged again? Will we, at some point, be two strangers no longer able to relate to each other at all? Sometimes I fear that erosion of our marriage is taking place with an alarming rapidity that neither of us knows how to halt. I anguish over the lost companionship Bill and I are denying ourselves because of our stubbornness (is that what it is?), because of our refusal to be vulnerable to each other for fear of rejection (yes, that's what it is—for me, anyway; I would rather not confront Bill for fear of being rejected). It's a cold loneliness—this indifference we pretend to feel toward each other. At least for me, it's pretending; maybe for him it's real. I hope not, because as long as we know we're pretending there is hope. I wish I knew the truth about our marriage. And I wish that I could start over again and do things right. But I can't, and I regret that.

Bill told me before we were married that he had a hard spot, a place where no one could go. I didn't believe him, feeling certain that my love for him would be able to penetrate any hardness.

Dad and I helped Gayle distribute commodities in Roseau, Warroad, and Badger this week. For our assistance, we were awarded a box of goodies containing peanut butter, egg mix, honey, canned pork, flour, butter and green beans. There is no strict monitoring at these giveaways—only a rarely looked at master list of people whose income is below a certain level—so pretty much anybody who wants free food can claim some. The people in Warroad were hungry and everything went; there were even stragglers who arrived too late to get any. In Roseau, however, and even more so in Badger, the allotted supply only dwindled until eventually we had to return some to be distributed next time (every three months). I can't help but think how different the situation would be in some place like Appalachia where people are in dire need. Roseau County is no hardship area; employment abounds and most people live quite comfortably. Our government works in mysterious ways.

Luella and Bingo Lil, the two elderly ladies who help Gayle distribute commodities in Roseau, are characters. Luella is four feet tall with a severe case of spine curvature that shortens her even more. Her job yesterday was to guard the door, and she executed her task with a soldier's ardor. I couldn't figure out her selection criteria but, whatever they were, she let most people in and kept only a few out.

Bingo Lil nurtures her passion seven nights a week. She's won the jackpot twice, and by last count reigned champion over so many tournaments that she's thinking of semi-retirement. She told me she plays in Roseau at the Elks and the Eagles, Steinbeck, Sprague, Warroad, and Greenbush. Following the bingo circuit is just the life for Lil whose job yesterday was bagging groceries. Bossiness took on new meaning when she was giving orders!

I had the pleasure of meeting Buddy, Gayle's most loyal commodities helper. Buddy has a mental handicap and a speech impediment. He adores Gayle and will work like a horse in order to receive his allotment of commodities that is twice the amount other volunteers get. He's very proud of his physical strength and couldn't resist a little teasing when he didn't think Dad lifted the boxes fast enough: "What's the matter, Mr. Pearson? Did you forget to eat your Cheerios this morning?" He also likes Rozie who frequently accompanies Gayle for a can of peanut butter. At one point, Gayle glanced in the back seat of her car to find Rozie and Buddy sharing a sucker—"It's my turn now, Wozie, and then yours." I thought Gayle was going to have a heart attack! When I asked Buddy if he was going to do commodities on Saturday, he said, "Saturday and Sunday are for fishing—no tommodities."

I wonder how people really feel about signing a sheet of paper in order to receive a bagful of groceries from the U.S. government. The old-timers probably don't give the event a second thought because they've been doing it for so long that it's become a reason for seeing old friends. But what about the young, single mother who came in to claim a bagful for herself and her five children? She averted my gaze as she signed her name, muttered a "thank you" while accepting a bag, and walked out with three of her kids in tow. When I asked Gayle about her, she said, "That woman has had so much adversity in her life, but she just keeps trying. I wish she'd get a break." I guess those few groceries were worth the brief discomfort (shame?).

Another young woman, a neighbor of ours, came in and talked with Gayle during the whole process, but without much enthusiasm. She answered Gayle's questions without volunteering any information beyond that which was solicited. I was surprised to see several people I knew while growing up receive their share. They never seemed poor to me, and I can't imagine what kind of need would force them to swallow their pride. Dad says that many are on Social Security, which is less than adequate to meet their needs. It was an even greater surprise to see a couple of people with office jobs (one worked for the government), but Gayle said they only make about $1000 a month.

I question where the real down-under, rock-bottom poor people are. I don't think I saw any. Gayle says that she transports commodities to those who are physically and/or financially unable to travel to one of the four locations. I have to wonder about those who don't read newspapers or listen to the radio, and are thus unaware of "commodity day." I guess Gayle reaches them, one way or another.

I wish I could say that I've never been exposed to abject poverty. I witnessed it many times during my tenure in Southeast Asia. I remember too vividly the wretchedness of the dwellings, the hunger and misery of the daily struggle to survive in the Philippines. Whoever said that there is dignity and freedom in poverty has never witnessed human suffering. The only freedom the poor have is the freedom to starve.

The human heart is the same all over the world, so to see human suffering—wherever it is happening—destroys me completely. Especially the children—thin arms and distended bellies and dark, sad eyes—make me feel sick with anger. I want to shout and shake my fists at all of the obscenely wealthy people in our country—the insufferably rich egomaniacs we're supposed to admire, the powerful leaders of rich countries, even the media. Who's responsible for enlightening those who don't know about poverty? Who's responsible for reviving the social conscience of those who know but don't care? Who's responsible for creating an understanding for those of us who know and care but can't make enough sense of the complexity to help? I used to believe that the sin God hates most is loss of faith, but now I think it's an unconcern and lack of love for the poor. A Christian who doesn't want to love everybody, to help those who need help, and to share what he/she has with those who have little or nothing, is guilty of the unpardonable sin. I can't understand how we as Americans can sleep at night, knowing that such poverty and hunger exist in parts of our world. How can we justify the salaries of CEOs and athletes? How do we explain Las Vegas? We need to be so much more generous and hospitable than we are.

One of my most profound beliefs is that God is in everyone—even those who don't believe in Him. And I feel close to God when I'm with poor people. But, except for The Peace Corps, I never seem to be able to stay, to make a long-term commitment to the poor. Something always seems to get in the way, such as selfishness and self-interest.

Everyone should do social service sometime in his life, the earlier the better. The Peace Corps and VISTA surely fulfill that responsibility. But the service need not be global or far-reaching. Rather, it can be a local commitment to help the poor in some setting, e.g., food kitchens, urban churches, teaching, even distributing commodities. It's important to be with people who are downtrodden and dispossessed, because being with them is the closest thing to "walking in the shoes." One can at least have a clue to what it means to not have enough of what a person needs. None of us can really change the world in our lifetimes, but is it not the case that all of us can touch the people around us in ways that may last?

I'm going to give my box of commodities to Mom and Dad. I felt no sense of guilt taking the groceries, since we ended up having to load many boxes and return them to Roseau again. There are too many people in this part of the country who just do not really need them. Why couldn't we give the extra groceries to the single mother and some of the others instead of having to return them?

After distributing commodities, Dad and I had coffee with Joyce and all of the Warroadites at the Patch and then again with Gayle at the Kozy Kitchen. We washed some clothes at the Laundromat and then headed out to Malung School where we visited Mom during her planning period for a while. When we finally arrived home, we feasted on homemade venison sausage before embarking on a long snocat ride.

My feelings about small town life are inconsistent and complicated. On a certain day I feel that I could never be happy in a small town and, in that literal sense, I've answered the question of whether I could ever go home again. On another day, however, I feel as if I'd trade the much-valued anonymity of city life for the warm security of a place where everyone knows at least the identity of everyone else. Even on those days though, I'm easily irritated at the conversations of people that center around the hockey rivalry between Roseau and Warroad, the weather or the latest divorce.

Roseau is a town of about 2500 people. According to the census, there hasn't been any significant population growth but the town continues to expand. Businesses thrive because people have money. The government recently forgave hundreds of farmers' loans in the country, an act that permitted the big farmers to buy more expensive machinery from local merchants. The downside of that act is that the small farmers are being shut out. Employment is high; even those eligible for commodities are far from destitute. Indeed, prosperity is evident wherever you go in Roseau.

In my observation (and also from my experience, having lived here through high school graduation), the people of Roseau seem to fall into two groups—and I describe them with some trepidation, for the descriptions will immediately invite argument and explanations of the exceptions, of which there are admittedly many. In the first group are sons who play hockey; daughters who are cheerleaders; children who go to college; and parents who clothes shop in the Twin Cities, vacation in Florida or out West and own cottages somewhere on Lake of the Woods. They are loyal to their town, so they supplement their wardrobe at local Burgraff's, own Polaris snocats, and attend the out-of-town hockey games.

The sons and daughters of the other group wrestle, and are active in FHA (Future Homemakers of America) or FFA (Future Farmers of America). They attend vocational/technical schools after high school to learn a trade, which they then use to find a job in Roseau or another small town. Their parents buy most of their clothes at JC Penney and work at Polaris. Their idea of a vacation is fishing on Lake of the Woods, summer and winter.

The similarities between the two groups (if, indeed, they do exist) are much greater than the differences, however. People in both groups are hard-working, honest, religious, and conservative in both their politics and social ideas. Extra-marital affairs, divorce, drinking, child custody battles, cancer, and car accidents are prevalent in a part of the country where the winters are hard and there's little to do beyond church, sports events, and the local VFW and Eagles Club—an environment not unlike that found in most small towns, I suspect.

Warroad is a smaller town twenty miles east of Roseau. It is Roseau's arch rival in hockey but the competition ends there. Warroad can't compete with Roseau in business, expansion, sophistication, and standard of living. Roseauites are somewhat contemptuous of the people in Warroad and the town itself. The Marvin family, northern Minnesota's only millionaires, built the town of Warroad and keeps it alive with its loyalty and generosity. While the people themselves are loyal to their town in many ways, they prefer to shop and work in Roseau or Thief River Falls.

What is probably the single most revealing factor of the attractiveness of both small towns is the high return of young people who want to raise their kids in these parts.

Attendance at a Roseau-Warroad hockey game leaves one both exhilarated and bemused. The fans are rabid, the noise deafening, the air intense, and the sideline comments disparaging. For the last four years Warroad has had the competitive edge and consistently emerged the victors. This year, the tables have turned and Roseau fans want revenge. When Roseau beat Warroad 9-0 in a game, the fans were disappointed that the score wasn't even more lopsided. Having fired their Warroad-born coach who hadn't been successful at defeating Warroad, Roseau now lauds the efforts of their new coach, forgetting that team development and the natural ability of the players might be playing just as important a role as the present coaching in their long-awaited success.

The male youth of Roseau and Warroad (and most of Northern Minnesota) are introduced to hockey at birth when they are presented with miniature hockey sticks and skates they'll grow into. At five, they are flawless skaters, ready to begin the hockey program which eventually weeds out the best, so that only a very small percentage of those "Squirts" are able to help their parents realize their dream of having a son play for the mighty Rams or Warriors.

I have to admit that I don't know what I'd do if I lived here and my boys wanted to play hockey (well, first they'd have to learn to skate a little better!). I'd like to think that I would try to change things a little, so that kids could play hockey more for the sheer pleasure of the sport and not be driven so much by pressure to be the best. Unfortunately, that pressure comes not only from the coaches but also from the parents. Just the other day I heard that when Roseau had Bantam tryouts this year, the coaches decided to have five lines on the A team. This left the B team with only two lines—not enough to play regulation games. The B team coach suggested that he take the fifth line of the A team and went so far as to identify the players who could switch over. Many of the parents were adamant in their refusal to allow this, however, stipulating that they would rather have their kid warm the bench on the A team than enjoy playing time on the B team. In all fairness, there was at least one parent who embraced the idea. Both she and her son wanted the "demotion" so he could play hockey. Their request was denied, ostensibly because he was too good.

Badger is a sleepy little town of about 800 people ten miles west of Roseau. Any changes that have occurred since I left 25 years ago are imperceptible. The town is the same size and the markings are all familiar—Hartz grocery store, a little more crowded now than it used to be; the Corner Café that serves cheeseburgers the way God meant them to taste (just enough grease to be juicy, toasted bun, fried onions, and pickles on the side); a gas station; the Catholic and Lutheran churches; and a town hall that accommodates every event from wedding dances to the distribution of commodities.

Badger holds a special place in my heart because my great uncle Iver, who recently died at 97, lived and farmed there all his life. He was known for his ramrod straight posture, business acumen, surly relationships with his brothers Sigurd and Joseph, and his brilliant dogs that he trained until they were almost human. "Rexy," he'd say, "I think it's time to get the cows in." Rex would respond immediately and, before Iver got to the barn, Rex would have rounded up the cows in the pasture and guided them to their individual stalls.

The best story I ever heard though was when Uncle Iver drove his car into a snow bank at the end of his long driveway and became firmly stuck. He yelled to Rex who was minding his own business back at the ranch, "Rex, bring me the shovel by the house." Without hesitation, as the story goes, Rex found the shovel—which was not by the house but in the shed—and brought it to Iver, balancing it in his mouth the whole way! Uncle Iver calmly rewarded him with a pat on the head. The story sounds apocryphal but my Dad says it's true, every detail.

Uncle Iver was a successful farmer until ten years before he died. Dad says Iver had a tremendous ego; that's what kept him going. He smoked, drank whiskey, and ate eggs and fat "all in moderation"—that was his key to a long life. His major character flaw, as far as I can tell, was his inability to get along with his brothers. Once when Uncle Sigurd was plowing, Uncle Iver walked out to the field to collect the money Sigurd owed him for land rental. Sigurd steered the tractor in Iver's direction, accelerated, and would have run him down if Iver hadn't run for his life!

Ten

We snocatted today and I was once again struck by my passion for the sport. The exhilaration I felt from another trip to Bemis Hill and back with my Dad and brother made me wish I were a poet so I could adequately describe the experience. It all starts with the air up here in Northern Minnesota—fragrant and so crisp it grabs you by the lungs and shakes you alive. Then there's the anticipation which can be painful if there is waiting involved, especially when the conditions are perfect, as they were today. Finally, there is the experience itself—like a story with a beginning, middle and end. As you walk to your snocat, you feel the snow crunch beneath your feet and hear the sound of the trail calling you. The smell of pine is intoxicating, and you can't wait to get going. You climb on your Arctic Cat and hit the starter. Its roar breaks the silence. You squeeze the throttle and the trail begins to disappear beneath you as your snocat swallows the snow so fast that the trees blur and your face stings. You feel like cheering. Just when you feel it's never going to stop, it does. The ride ends and you're back home, removing your gloves and wondering if there isn't some way you could make a career out of snocatting.

What do I enjoy most about snocatting? Speeding over a snow-covered field and mastering the roller coaster bumps and corners of a trail are unbelievably thrilling. But my favorite kind of ride is the one I take right before sunset with one of my sons. I like to time the event so that just as we enter a particular opening on our favorite tree-lined trail, the sky fires up and intensifies until I think it's going to burst. We ride the rest of the way home in the afterglow. When we arrive we both pause to take one last, lingering look at the fading phenomenon that will soon settle into an orange and pink bed and then disappear completely. I feel warm and happy. That's snocatting at its best.

Dad took Rozie and Jon to Roseau with him—he'll wait while they attend story hour at the library—so I'm enjoying all by myself the quiet serenity and satisfaction that the state of aloneness can bring, especially in the country. The day is custom made—trees clothed in the white garments of new-fallen snow, unblemished blue skies, warm sunshine, crisp air filled with the songs of well-fed birds, and an occasional raucous cry of crows. I am content, sated, and in perfect tune with my surroundings.

I do believe that the world was a lot simpler and more secure when I graduated from high school in the early 60s, and then it changed. We were prepared for a relatively uncomplicated society. We believed in the work ethic, government, and God—all of the important ideas our parents upheld and promulgated. Things were relatively unambiguous. There were good guys and bad guys; issues were, for the most part, black and white. Then our relatively uncomplicated society took on a different appearance: The issues became more multi-colored and mixed with shades of gray. At least that's what happened in my part of the world where, admittedly, the times didn't change as quickly as they did in some other parts.

I think that part of what kept the issues simple, before the tumultuous sixties gained steam, was the fact that we didn't spend a lot of time examining our prejudices, hang-ups, and naiveté. These things existed, of course, but here in the North Country it was pretty easy to not recognize them, or, if recognized, ignore them. We believed that our lives were pretty much guaranteed, that we were living the unadulterated good life. Then the Civil Rights Movement and Vietnam became huge problems for my generation, and we couldn't keep our heads in the sand any longer. Maybe it's the case that the problems we faced twenty-five years ago were just more concrete than the fears we are living with today. Or maybe that's a naïve statement in itself.

When the kids got off the bus, Wayne, Dad and I took them up to Bemis Hill on the snocats. They did some sledding but the wind was strong and cold. On the way home, Willie was so enthralled with the sunset that he wasn't paying attention to his driving responsibility and ran into the stopped snocat ahead of us. By mutual agreement, he is not allowed to drive the snocat for the rest of the week. I didn't want to come down too hard on him, because a few days ago he drove to Dewey's with the gang to pick up the Sunday paper, and he was proud of his accomplishment.

Will decided to quit basketball because he wasn't enjoying the practices very much and wanted to spend more time snocatting and just fooling around with his cousins. I wasn't surprised. I think it was a good decision, especially since calving season is almost here and he will want to be around to participate. Basketball just took up too much of his time.

Zach is still playing hockey and loving it, but his situation is so different from Willie's. He practices only twice a week and seldom has games. He has a tournament coming up and I can't wait. He and I were talking about the tournament and he said, "Maybe I'll even make a goal this time!" It's hard to compete with the kids who have been playing hockey almost all their lives, but Zach hangs in there and enjoys the challenge.

I'm smiling just thinking about an incident that took place soon after we arrived. It was before one of Zach's hockey games in Warroad. I was feeling especially solicitous, so I accompanied him to the locker room where I proceeded to help him get dressed and padded along with all the other little boys (and a few mothers). I was enjoying all of the game conversation when my attention was suddenly turned to the corridor where a high school hockey player was whistling a happy tune as he made his way to the locker room—stark naked! Our eyes met, his head immediately dropped three feet, and he ran the rest of the way, doing his best to cover up. I exited with a red face amid a chorus of youthful laughter, including Zach's, vowing never to return to a boys' locker room.

Both boys received letters from their friends at home. They were happy about that even though they tried to appear nonchalant. Willie and Zach continue to miss Bill and their friends, but they told me they didn't want to go home until the scheduled time—at the end of March. (I don't know why I need to keep hearing that from them.) In Zach's letter he learned that his soccer team has started practicing indoors, and that information left him feeling wistful, but he rationalized that he will do just fine without the indoor practice. School relationships have improved for both boys—I don't hear much anymore—and they appear to be having a good time.

What really cements their desire to stay is the fun they have with their cousins, both at home and at different extracurricular activities. Life is very relaxing. They get home from school at 4:20, have a snack while watching a cartoon at Grandpa and Grandma's, snocat or play, and then eat supper and do homework. Willie loves Wednesday Release Time and Youth Group at the Covenant Church. He thinks Pastor Joe is great and apparently the feeling is mutual. Zach enjoys Adventure Club on Wednesday nights but feels a little cheated because he thinks his evenings aren't as fun-filled as Willie's. Both are doing well in school and with piano lessons.

Jonathan! Oh, he's having the time of his life. My thoughts frequently turn now to the void in his life that Rozie will leave when we return to Toledo. Those two are inseparable; they're so busy playing school and office that they live in a little world of their own. Jon's first thought in the morning and his last at night is of Rozie. Their latest interest is journal writing, I think because they see me writing in my journal. Every time we go someplace, they confer to decide what they should take along—a suitcase of "homework," their "journals," a stuffed animal or doll, and a favorite book. They take very seriously their responsibility of helping Grandpa feed the cows and water Si, the bull. If they miss the event, they feel as if they've let Grandpa down. Jon still misses Bill, especially at night, but he doesn't cry anymore.

Twenty-five years ago, after high school graduation, I left the part of the country I grew up in to become a wanderer and story collector. For the next ten years I had a love affair with the world that took me from Bemidji State University, where I was a political activist and McCarthy campaigner; to the East Coast where I taught school in Connecticut, discovered New York, frequented the Cape, skied in Vermont, thrilled to the freedom of sky diving, and generally lived recklessly and with the kind of abandonment that can be enjoyed only when you're young, ambitious, and unencumbered. Feeling restless after two years of living in the East, I joined The Peace Corps and spent the next two years spreading American good will (and feeding my appetite for adventure) in the Philippines and Southeast Asia. After satisfying my wanderlust with innumerable memorable experiences in that part of the world (including meeting my future husband in Thailand), I returned to the University of Minnesota to begin graduate work. I married Bill, earned my doctorate, and took a job at The University of Toledo where I am presently working. I have three boys who are 11, 9, and 5 years old. As I am writing, I'm on sabbatical from the University, living once again on my parents' farm in Northern Minnesota. My husband remains in Toledo where we will join him in April. Why, at the age of 43 (no longer young and unencumbered, but still ambitious!), did I choose to return to my small, rural community which, for me, had long ago become a place to be from, not a place to be?

During my years of wanderlust, I had fancy jobs and no jobs, lived in youth hostels and spacious apartments, struck up friendships in war zones and various addresses. I loved it all. But no matter my monetary circumstances, I often felt homesick and nostalgic for all things familiar, for the safety of my parents and the place they lived. And, in time, I decided to settle down because I wanted a family like the one I grew up with. Besides, I had met Bill.

Even after deciding to settle down though, I knew that circumstances dictated a place far from home. I had left small town, rural life forever. So what brought me back, made me decide to spend four months of my well-earned sabbatical on the farm without my husband? There were the boys, of course. But for me, personally, I think it was my accumulated romanticized version of life in the country that kept growing over the years. It could also have been a yearning to rid myself of weariness by returning to the simple life. I built up a strong desire to watch hockey games again, ice fish, snowmobile, and make hearty stews and cornbread. I wanted to spend lazy days with my father, have intimate conversations with my mother, and get to know my siblings and their spouses. Then there were the Minnesota skies. My memory of and anticipation for Minnesota sunsets and bright stars close to the earth were so great that on my first night here, I stared at the sky and let the familiar warmth envelope me. I wondered if there could ever be a winter night sky as beautiful as that of Northern Minnesota. Not even the Filipino sunsets were as splendid.

I've always thought of this farm as the place to go when my emotional needs are the greatest. The farm is my sanctuary. In graduate school there were times when the strain was so great I had to go home to regain some kind of objectivity in my life. The danger of being totally committed to academia is that you lose sight of the basic things in life, the places and people who are truly important to you, and focus instead on superficial activities and goals that are all-consuming. During those times, I had to go home to a place where the surroundings, the activity, the work and play—the whole atmosphere—was completely different from that which was consuming me day after day. I remember trying to explain this to my parents—how I didn't go home to please them, although I knew they were always happy to see me, but to save my soul, which was often lost in academic affairs. I had to rediscover those things in life that were truly important and indispensable to my happiness. Sometimes, my rejuvenation would take only a couple of days. Other times, I needed to stay longer to feel sufficiently strengthened and rested.

Always, I cried when I left the farm. When Bill went home with me, leaving wasn't so bad. He would comfort me for the first few miles after we left so I didn't cry much beyond Skime. When I went home by myself, however, I remained more or less teary all the way back to Minneapolis.

I have to take to the farm every year. When I'm here I know, truly know, the values of a day.

With only one month to go, I don't regret my decision to come home for a while. I've had a lot of time to think about my life, and I've learned some things about myself. I'm enjoying hockey, snocatting and ice fishing, just as I knew I would. My parents' and brother's appreciation for the stews and cornbread in itself makes my stay worthwhile. I love the long days spent with my father and the stolen moments with my mother. My siblings and their spouses are fun and interesting, each in his/her own right. The sunsets and the stars are as awesome as ever. Last but not least, I will have some stories to tell and memories to store—being the memory collector I am.

Eleven

Being a college student in the 60s meant feeling passionate about everything: Vietnam, Civil Rights, God, love, music—there was so much going on that it was hard to decide on a focus for my passion. It so happened that I was elected to serve on the Executive Council of the Student Senate in college, and I did everything I could to deserve the honor. So when I was asked to attend the National Student Association (NSA) Congress as a senior, I was ecstatic. The theme of the Congress was the Student Power Movement. During the 60s students had no control over their college environment; in fact, college was just an extension of high school with the Dean of Students acting like a parent—*in loco parentis,* as it were. The NSA felt strongly that students should have a voice in the educational process that they and their parents were paying for. They believed that students had the right to decide what time they should come in at night and what they should do in their dormitories, as well as what should be done with the fees they had to pay—in short, they should be able to determine how they will run their lives while living on campus. I believed all of this too, so it wasn't hard for me to be passionate about student power.

That year the Congress was in College Park, Maryland. The Students for Democratic Society (SDS) was a powerful organization at that time, and it threatened to upset the Congress with its untoward and outrageous behavior. I have to smile, twenty years later, at my naiveté. I persuaded the entire Minnesota delegation to walk out of the assembly when Timothy Leary was doing his hallucinogenic thing on stage. The live Saran Wrap Commercial was just too much for my socially conservative tastes. Anyway, the NSA awakened me to a whole new world, and I couldn't suppress my enthusiasm when I returned to campus. When I tried to explain to the rest of the Student Senate what my week had been like, I came off sounding "bubbly"—not a great compliment during those times when passionate people were supposed to be intense and serious.

The next year my friend Jim, who was president of the Student Senate after I graduated, attended the same Congress—this time in Manhattan, Kansas. Jim wrote to me in Connecticut where I was teaching and said that so much was packed into those twelve days he was there that he wondered if it was even possible to explain the week to someone who had never had the experience and could not appreciate it—hence, his letter to me.

Compared to Maryland, Jim said, the Kansas experience was mild. The SDS, while pervasive as usual, didn't cause anyone to walk out and the food was good, thanks to me (I complained about the food so much the year before that the food service director at the University of Maryland was fired, and NSA pledged to provide acceptable food at future Congresses).

Jim and Jack, another delegate, drove to Salina, Kansas from Bemidji and then took the bus the rest of the way. To quote from Jim's letter, "the cornfields were endless, broken only by an occasional wind-bruised house and telephone wires . . . . With gray skies and dull green corn, the drive was all quite depressing—but not nearly as depressing as the bus ride." They left Salina in the early morning darkness, "the bus falling quickly into the rhythm of the road winding through the low hills. By 6:30 dawn had arrived and it was light, but it was an eerie green-yellow light that filtered heavily through the trees like some strange sickness. As we entered Fort Riley, the military cemetery greeted us—thousands and thousands of simple white crosses neatly rowed over the recently cut grass and bathed in that awful light. Death's gloom was everywhere—I could see it, feel it, and breathe it—and what I thought while standing there was like a terrible nightmare."

At the Congress, Jim said that he immediately became involved with a series of role play situations designed to teach and develop the kind of leadership necessary for the student governments that they hoped would be flowering on campuses across the land. But he was surprised and dismayed that so many so-called student leaders were, what he called "authoritarian egoists," more concerned with preserving their position and influence in the system, i.e., the status quo, than in using their power to improve the lot of the college student. On top of that (which was quite enough to wreck the Student Power Movement, I would think), Jim said they didn't appear to even understand student power, something that he could hardly abide. Everyone spoke of a bright future for college students—one that included no rules for dorm living, etc, but Jim felt that, unless some of the leaders changed, the picture would always be one of continuing to talk of a bright future from a dark present.

At the same time the NSA Congress was going on in Kansas, the Chicago bloodbath was all over TV. Tom Hayden, the organizer of the demonstrations, was in attendance at the Congress and Jim spent some time with him. He said that even there in Kansas, a thousand miles from Chicago, Tom Hayden was being harassed! As they walked downtown, a car always followed a block back, and when they passed a parked car, Tom looked in the windows to see if anyone was lying on the floor, waiting for him to pass. When Jim wrote me this, all I could think of was what a police state we seem to live in. Anyone who dissents invites being crushed or otherwise silenced, like in Chicago. What I saw on television at the time reminded me of a film I had seen of Berlin in 1940. I could see the streets smeared with blood. And for what? Why were we so scared of seeing 40,000 people demonstrating against that horrible war in Vietnam? It all left me very confused and depressed. I remember thinking that if we're not already in a police state, we seemed to be evolving into one.

On a lighter note, my involvement in the Student Power Movement spawned a romance that made 1967 a very good year indeed. The vice president of NSA that year took a liking to me—joining me in Ashland, Wisconsin for the McCarthy campaign, encouraging me to travel to Washington for an infrequent visit, and inviting me to have dinner at his parents' house in Chapel Hill. I accepted the dinner invitation and, to show my gratitude, accidentally spilled crème de menthe on the beautiful Spanish tablecloth that adorned the dining room table. It was, needless to say, a most embarrassing moment that I think resulted in the termination of my relationship with an interesting guy.

It was easy being a political activist in the 60s because protests and sit-ins were a relative novelty and people paid attention. Now we're so jaded that protests draw very little attention. Maybe the causes also have something to do with the lack of interest.

I am an early riser. I like getting up with the sun. The brief moments before daybreak are mine, with no intrusion, and I cherish them. I like the dawn of a crisp, cold day when winter blesses the land with its first benediction of silent snow. I also like a soft, spring morning when I feel the earth growing . . . and a summer daybreak when dew-festooned webs capture the first sunshine . . . and the beginning of a cool, colorful autumn day. Living in a place where there are four seasons offers the best possible life because there is so much anticipation. I can honestly say that I look forward to every season with excitement and hope. Even winter, the season dreaded by so many who live here in the frigid North Country, is welcome because it offers the promise of rest—no grass to mow, flowers to tend, and gardens to worry about. You can sit back and watch nature sleep. When I lived in the Philippines, the thing I missed most, aside from my family, was the changing of the seasons. It seemed there was no time for my body to change course.

I faithfully set the alarm clock every night only to turn it off the next morning before it rings. My inborn clock never fails. I guess it's because I'm eager to wake up—I feel an excitement and a sense of urgency to meet the day head-on. I have a plaque on my wall. It says, "This day is yours with all its possibilities. Each minute, each hour, is a gift of life that is yours for the taking." I don't want to waste any of it, especially now, here, where there is so much to do.

I dress quickly, checking the weather through the kitchen window. Last night's frost starched the trees so they stand tall and lovely, glistening with white crystals. There is no wind . . . the ice-touched branches hang motionless. For a few seconds I am fascinated by the beauty and perfection of nature's artwork. Then, mindful that the sun is ready to rise and the precious daybreak hours are fast approaching (and the kids will be up soon), I open the door to let Charlie out for his morning constitution.

As winter melts into spring, Northern Minnesotans begin waiting patiently for the signs of vibrant new life. I think there is great wonder in this time of year, just before spring arrives. Our senses are tuned to the subtle changes around us—longer days, the gradual warming of the sun's rays, the sights and sounds of the first birds returning from their migrations, the steady retreat of a season's worth of tired snow. Here on the farm we wait for our own signs of spring: running water in Bear Creek, snow melting in the ditches, the return of the Canada geese and Sand Hill Cranes, and the occasional hawk swooping down to investigate new discoveries.

It's a season of wonder . . . and waiting . . . . and patience. In no other part of the world do wonder, waiting, and patience pay off so greatly than in Northern Minnesota.

I've been missing Bill terribly these days, but it's not the sweet kind of sorrow that comes from two people knowing that, except for distance, everything is fine in their lives, and when the temporary separation is over, life will resume normal togetherness. I've had that kind of sorrow with Bill, and reunification was wonderful. One of the best examples of this sorrow-reunification love was when we had to live apart for a year right after we got married. Another is the year's separation we endured when he had to stay in Thailand while I studied at The University of Minnesota. Letters just weren't enough to sustain that long-distance relationship, especially one that had not had time to grow. What kept me faithful more than anything else was my family, especially my mother who kept reminding me that Bill was worth waiting for. When I questioned her authority in that matter, since she had not yet met Bill, she related (again!) the enthusiastic letters I wrote home about him while I was still with him in Thailand. She would say, "You couldn't have possibly told us the things you did if you weren't head-over-heels in love with him. It's different this time, so you be good!" It didn't hurt her perception of Bill when I told her that he was old-fashioned and firmly believed that marriage is for keeps. I knew that Mom would like to hear that, especially when she told me how worried she and Dad were about what Bill would think of them and their meager homestead. It turns out that Mom need never have worried about Bill's reaction to them and the farm. He genuinely and truly loved my parents, and every member of my family, from the very first and that love has never wavered.

The sadness I feel over his absence now is a kind of depression formed from the knowledge that all is not right between us, and that reunification will only force us to face the truth about our relationship. If there is an ebb and flow to life, I am definitely in the ebb part of the cycle—feeling pretty low. But, as cycles go, the flow will return and when it does, I'll feel happy again. I'll experience the joy that endures through the bad times. All will be well. I have to believe this. I'm a Pollyanna.

I'm told there are professional people around who help married couples fight cleanly. I wonder how they do it. Our fights are explosions that clear the air (is that "clean"?), occasionally redefine issues, and sometimes re-establish genuine contact with one another, but they are never unemotional—more so on my part than on Bill's. We say terrible things to each other and then feel that it's too late to apologize. The way out of a stalemate is often the way through conflict. I wish we wouldn't fight, but the worst times are when we don't fight. At least when we fight, we communicate. Sometimes I precipitate a fight just to get somewhere.

At a party just before I left Sylvania, several of us were discussing the right way to deal with the bad things that happen in our life. A good friend of mine theorized that most of what happens to us—even the negative—is part of the richness of life and should be treated as such. He acknowledged that very bad things, such as violent crime, should be treated differently, of course, and should warrant our anger. But things such as the loss of a job or tough times in a marriage should be stored in that part of our mind that tells us to accept the bad along with the good. I remember thinking that he can be cavalier about adversity, since he's had so little of it in his life. The same goes for me.

So, I accept the rough spots in our marriage. And yet, I have to say, for the record (which suddenly seems to be very important), that we are happy a lot of the time. When things are bad, something always seems to break up my melancholia. Maybe my sabbatical is, in fact, at least partly about my marriage. Maybe both Bill and I needed it to rethink our commitment.

I have made a firm resolve. I will discard all previously held notions about the way things and people ought to be and are not. Bill is as he is—he cannot think as I do, much less feel the way I feel. It is time for me to relinquish all immature expectations of him. The same holds for him. He will have to learn to accept me the way I am now—learn to see me as I really am, not the way I was and not as he wants me to be. When I return home, I'm going to work on my marriage as I've never done before.

When I was about to leave San Pablo, Philippines, I thought every day about how much shorter the time was before I went home. As excited as I was about the prospect of being reunited with my family though, the thought of leaving also filled me with regret. I knew that I was leaving a place and people I had grown to love for good and for always. It was as irrevocable as death. I kept assuring myself that I would return someday and visit. But I also knew that once I left, I would never really go back. That kind of thinking made the thought of leaving a very sad one; but the overriding impression, the one that I felt 80% of the time, was of a need to get home, to start building a new life.

In his book, *The Floating Opera*, Barth talks about a showboat that goes up and down a river with a play on its decks. The audience sits on the banks and watches the play go by. Since the boat is moving and the people on the shore are stationary, each person sees only small snatches of the play. When the boat comes back down the river individuals pick up on it again, perhaps relating, perhaps not, depending on how much or little has happened while the play is out of sight. People pick up on it again, however, only if they themselves have not moved on. I think our lives are like that. We meet people and interact with them for as long as our courses are parallel. Then we separate, perhaps for a long time, maybe just a short time, or forever. If it has been an especially long time, we find that we have a hard time picking up again—unless our respective "plays" are highly similar. Of course, there's always the chance that we will become so involved in a play that we will pick up and follow it, but that's hard, for we must keep up with the boat and ignore the myriads of other plays that are traveling in different directions and at different speeds along that same river.

Today, the river seems to be jammed, and the total number of "plays" available and passing us is of such proportions that we are almost unaware of most of them. It's sad. People don't have time to settle, to be steady. There are simply too many forces, opportunities and experiences pulling us in different directions. As a result, we bounce sort of aimlessly like children in a big candy shop, running so fast from one counter to another and stuffing our mouths and chewing with such desperate haste that we don't even have a chance to enjoy one piece for fear of missing our chances at the others.

Interpersonal relationships are becoming more and more transient. This is nobody's fault. It's simply that first, we don't expect relationships to last very long, and second, people themselves are transient today, moving from city to city, state to state, even to other countries. Finally, the opportunities that life presents are myriad and so pressing that we literally don't have time for friends who aren't in easy reach.

I wonder if others agree that it's relatively easy to attack and expound more or less effectively on the big theoretical problems and detach ourselves from the day-to-day problems.

Twelve

I'm sitting in Mom's classroom watching her conduct a reading lesson with her first graders. She modified the thought question at the end of the story that asks children what they like to do at the ocean. Knowing that none of her students has ever been to the ocean, nor would they be likely to go, she asked them what they like to do at the lake. That question generated all kinds of enthusiastic responses.

The children are respectful and considerate of each other. Five of the seven second graders took turns reading books to me and, even though the other two children in the group had probably already read the book, they listened intently for a while as if they had never heard the story before. Then they read a book together and collaborated on a written summary. While the second graders were reading to me, or to each other, Mom was conducting a lesson for the first graders, except for three children who were working on their paper mache penguins in a corner of the room. One little girl needed help so another jumped up and quietly provided some assistance. The children moved around the room freely and purposefully. When one needed individual attention from the teacher, the rest of the class either waited quietly or, if the interruption took time, they worked on their art project. There was a lot of productive noise but no major disruptions. I know now why Mom still has to prepare after 30 years of teaching—she needs to be incredibly

119

organized in order to monitor all of the instructional activities and concerns of the children. I also know why she's tired when she gets home at 6:30.

The longer I'm married the more I'm convinced that relationships are all about expectations. When two people do what the other expects, their lives run smoothly. Sooner or later, though, someone makes a mistake, or maybe desperately moves in the opposite direction, and things go wrong. The relationship becomes increasingly distant until there is either a physical separation or a cold silence. Both situations are intolerable, especially if one partner still loves. I think that separation has to be preferable to the cold silence, but it's not always possible, e.g., when children are involved.

I know there are people who are capable of mature development in mind and spirit apart from an intimate and permanent commitment to another person, but I am not one of them. I have learned and experienced and assimilated more through my relationship with Bill than through any other avenue I can think of. Then why is our relationship so painful much of the time? Why do we love each other and have the partnership of mind and heart and body when we're separated but fight when we're together?

Bill and I both seem to react, in situations where we are angry at each other, not to the facts, but to some stereotype of, or preconceived notion as to what the other thinks. Like most stereotypes or preconceptions there is enough truth in each to keep it alive, but it is probably 90% false. For instance, he "knows" ahead of time how things are going to go: He snaps or vents some frustration at me, either because of something related to me or because I happen to be in the way. I take it personally; he tries to apologize; I reject the apology because, to my way of thinking, he is merely apologizing for some particular incident, which is only a manifestation of a larger problem for which I consider him not apologetic at all. He, on the other hand, thinks it is important not to drag a whole lot of baggage into what is really a discrete event, and gets frustrated all over again by the fact that he has to deal with a cosmic problem every time some minor mishap occurs. Given these synergistic, self-amplifying preconceptions, it is hardly surprising that most of our spats turn into a relational Armageddon!

Bill and I don't say "I'm sorry" often enough, even though we're aware of the power of those words. We used to say them a lot—after every fight—but they're increasingly absent from our lives now.

I'm easily hurt. Bill says that I'm too sensitive. What does that mean, exactly? Isn't hurt a legitimate response to disappointment and shouldn't it be expressed? If I don't express it, it turns to anger and resentment and then I attack.

I'm afraid to face a painful truth of what I might learn about myself from Bill. And, since he's stingy with both criticism and compliments, I hardly have to worry about him telling me!

I'm certain Bill knows I love him, both as a husband and father and as one of the most remarkable and truly generous people I have ever known. And I know he loves me. This is the rock of everything. This is the reality which sees us through all our years—the stress and strain of two very different people united in marriage, with all the normal struggles of bearing and raising children and defining and redefining their own identities at the same time. I believe that God meant for Bill and me to be together. I really believe that.

The reality of God is the foundation of everything I believe. As long as that reality can be affirmed honestly, I am satisfied that somewhere, somehow, the meaning of it all will be clear. Between the options of a world created by freakish chance and the option of a God whose love extends to all creation, ever drawing us toward meaning and purpose, I choose the latter. But there's the freedom that goes along with meaning and purpose. In a universe where real good is possible, real evil must be possible too. Therefore, I'm unwilling to blame God for serious illness or awful accidents—and I certainly don't blame Him for my troubled marriage.

I struggle with the hard questions Christianity poses. The most difficult of all is the question of how God can be both omnipotent and compassionate. If He is omnipotent and compassionate he could, and would, eradicate evil, but since He doesn't do that, logic says that He either lacks compassion or is powerless. I know that God is neither of these.

I remember a Christmas a few years back when my Uncle Ed was still alive. He wrote us a letter where he summarized, with simplicity and clarity, the Christian faith. I keep that letter in my Bible to remind me, when I want to complicate my faith, that it really isn't so difficult after all. Part of his letter reads like this: *Yes, Christmas is the day on which we celebrate the most important event that ever took place on this old earth—the birth of our Lord and Savior, Jesus Christ. His coming made it possible for each and every one of us to have our sins forgiven. And to know that some day when our journey on this old earth comes to an end, we will be going to a far better place. According to the Bible, all who trust in Him as their own personal Lord and Savior are to inherit eternal life. Yes, the greatness and wonder of it all is far too much for me to comprehend. However, we do not have to understand it all. It says in the Good Book that we are saved by grace through faith, and through no merits of our own. How wonderful it is going to be someday to be in that wonderful place, where there will be no more pain and suffering of any kind. It is also wonderful to know that it will be a place where sin cannot enter in—sin that destroys both body and soul and causes untold remorse and regret. Well, I think I'd better bring this letter to an end. I hope that all of your family, Judy, will accept Christ as their personal Savior, if they haven't already done so . . . . and I hope that you can read this scribbling.*

Sincerely in Christ, Uncle Ed

Dad, Roz, Jon, and I spent the day with Joyce while she made her weekly Weight Watchers round in Northern Minnesota. The whole experience was an endurance test. I set the alarm for 2:45 a.m. (yes, in the morning) but, as usual, beat the alarm clock and awakened at 2:30; so I got up, made coffee, showered, threw my laundry together and woke the kids. We were on the road at 3:50 and met Joyce at Sharon and Shawn's a little before 4:30. When we arrived in International Falls two hours later, Joyce went to her first meeting at 6:45 while we all had coffee at Hardy's. We met Joyce at the Holiday Inn at 8:30 and, while the rest went to Pamida to buy her a VCR, I went downtown to re-familiarize myself with stores I had frequented the summer after high school when I worked at the A & W Drive-In. We met again at 10:30, deposited my dirty clothes at the Laundromat, and drank coffee at Bridgeman's while the clothes washed. At 11:30 Joyce had her second meeting so Dad, the kids, and I drove around again for a while and visited my cousin Jean at the telephone office where she has worked for 25 years. We then spent some time at the library until Joyce met us at 1:30. At this point, the realization that the day was just a little more than half over hit me like a rock, and I began wondering if it would ever end. We had lunch at Hardy's and headed out to Little Fork where Joyce had her third meeting of the day at 3:00. Our primary source of excitement in that tiny logging town was watching the heavy traffic on Main Street—Boise Cascade mill workers using Little Fork as a short cut, I guess. We rushed to Baudette for Joyce's final meeting of the day at 5:00. Roz and Jon were sound asleep finally. To pass the time, Dad and I drove across the river to tour Rainy River in Canada. Mildly exhausted, we picked up Joyce and arrived in Warroad about 7:30 and at home a little after 8:00. I did mention that this was an endurance test! I don't know how she does it every week. But it was fun spending time with Joyce and exploring old landmarks in familiar territory.

Thirteen

It's because of Bill that I was able to complete my masters and my doctorate degrees in four years. He spent many hours helping me conceptualize difficult theoretical issues, and we had fun working together to solve a problem.

I remember one time in particular when I was preparing for my oral preliminary exam, and I couldn't reconcile two different models of the reading process that accounted for explaining the size of the perceptual span in reading. I remember feeling that I was so close to an explanation but couldn't get all of the details to fall into place. The night before the exam, Bill stayed up with me until I had an explanation that I felt was strong and better than anything that could be found in the research literature.

As it turned out, the exam was a lot easier than I expected. In fact, I felt that my answers were much better than the questions. The committee members had not, it seemed to me, done their homework, and it was obvious they had read my paper only cursorily. Finally, when only twenty minutes remained, and I was growing more frustrated all of the time because I hadn't been given a chance to perform, I boldly asked my professors if they weren't interested in how I reconciled the two competing theories. Taken somewhat by surprise, they encouraged me to go on, and I proceeded to present a model of the reading process that did a fairly good job of reconciling the different viewpoints espoused by leading researchers in the field. When I finished, they were obviously pleased, and I felt great. Bill and I celebrated that night, spending more money on dinner than we could afford!

One particular stumbling block for me in graduate school was Statistics. I had a complete mental block when it came to understanding the concept of probability! Then when I finally got the hang of it, with a little help from Bill (who tossed coins for me in a Dinkytown café), I ultimately decided that it wasn't very difficult after all, and that figuring it out was not any huge accomplishment. For proof of that "fact", I took as evidence my own mastery! In short, anything I did was *ipso facto* no particular accomplishment. I even felt that way about earning my PhD—if I could do it, anyone could.

Now I sometimes feel the need to prove that what I've accomplished so far with my life is significant, but to do so would be trying to prove that my children don't exist. Will, Zach, and Jon are my three greatest accomplishments. They give me clarity of purpose that I don't have with anything else I do in my life. Even more than The Peace Corps, my sons make me feel that what I am doing is exactly what I am supposed to be doing at this moment in time. Why is it then that I don't think I deserve any of the credit for helping them become what they are and what they will be?

Despite its inestimable value, doing a decent job of raising children, being a good friend, helping my family, teaching, and making people happy—in short, all of the things that I think I'm doing quite well and consistently—do not attract a lot of attention on the world stage. They are valuable accomplishments, but they are not the sorts of things that have an immediate impact on the "world." No one sits up and takes notice. I don't want to be fed platitudes about everybody not being able to be a big deal or that one should be satisfied with one's niche in life—hollow and condescending sentiments. But a part of me wants to accomplish something that tells the world now and in the future, "Look, World, I exist(ed)!"

Every possibility in life excludes others. In order to be an earthmover, I would not be able to be me. And basically I like myself. Striving to be the best mother, daughter, sister, friend, and teacher—the intangible accomplishments—is giving me introspection, sensitivity to others and an equanimity that I would not willingly trade. It's made me a happy person. Ernest Hemingway accomplished great things but he killed himself. I don't mean to imply that famous/rich/powerful people are never happy. That sentiment is certainly trite and arguably untrue. Nevertheless, the obsession that greatness requires carries with it its own costs. And, while I would like the greatness, I'm not at all certain that on a balance I would be any more satisfied.

In many ways, the appeal of religion rests on the promise that if there's a place for us in Heaven there's no need for us to be remembered here. As a Christian, I believe that, but believing it doesn't take away the nagging feeling that I should be doing something extraordinary. Ultimately, though, I think the answer must lie in concentrating on the here and now: living the present to the fullest and simply accepting the fact of mortality. I say that, not because it resolves any pain at the prospect of obscurity, but simply because, unless that is the frame of mind we adopt, we run the risk of losing, or not appreciating, the moment. That answer is not very satisfying but it's all I can think of.

Undoubtedly, the hardest thing about living—at least about reflective living—is learning to reconcile oneself to the fact not only of death but of being forgotten. It has to be done, and there is no way to rationalize the awfulness of it. It must simply be accepted. The true tragedy, however, in not doing so is that it deprives that which remains of much of its joy.

I wonder what kind of relationship I will have with my sons one day. What I want is a relationship that is close and endearing, and they may be afraid of that kind of thing. Also there is the feeling, childish but natural (I think), that I will become somehow anachronistic, and that what young men take for foolish sentimentalism in mothers (and I can be sentimental to a fault) should be tolerated but not really enjoyed. I probably will feel insecure in my relationship with my sons: Will they value and appreciate me? I don't think it will be a matter of love—I hope they'll love me—but love can be a most degrading thing if handled wrong, for it can be horribly self-centered and condescending.

I've heard it said that a mother cannot take her child seriously—his ideas and thoughts are just too simple, too lacking in experience and understanding to be seriously pondered by an adult mind. As the child grows and matures, though, and his perception deepens and his understanding increases, the mother is forced to take him more and more seriously, until finally they're able to speak together on a plane where age ceases to be important, where both can learn from each other. That's what I want to have happen—age ceasing to be a factor and my sons and I becoming equal.

Someday my sons will be unalterably and forever gone. They will be far beyond my grasp, as a mother. I have to accept this; it can't be any other way. This wouldn't be a problem if I had lived fifty years ago when children didn't leave much. But transience has entered the picture, and the days of Grandma Rosie, ruling with matriarchal splendor over a brood of progeny spanning 70 years, are but a memory. I have this feeling that by the time I become a grandmother, grandmothers just won't have strong familial obligations anymore!

For 24 years I will provide clothing, food, guidance, support, love, care, tenderness, and all the things a mother can give to her children. I will teach them about compassion, integrity, about doing what's right. (I want them not only to do well, but to do good.) I will encourage them to select experiences that challenge them, not just do things the easy way. But my sons will leave home, become independent and gradually lose the need for these services. And I wouldn't want it any other way. It makes me nervous though, knowing that someday I will have to demand their respect and love on a different plane, the same plane on which I receive love and respect from my friends. I wonder if my sons will want my wisdom.

I helped in Mom's classroom again. It's such a pleasant place to spend time! The first graders read to me today. You can tell they've been taught to read with a heavy emphasis on phonics because they could decode any word that conformed to the rules. They also comprehended well, as evidenced by their ability (and enthusiasm) for retelling the story. I was impressed.

I had a teacher lounge conversation with Charlie Klotz who is the fifth and sixth grade teacher and principal. His dissatisfaction with the two-grade classroom is so great that he has applied for a job in Roseau. He said that if he could have only one grade, he would stay here in Malung because he enjoys the small school atmosphere. I wonder how that problem will be resolved. It's interesting to compare his views with those of my mother.

Jon and Roz visited school with me today. They pretended they were students and "studied" very hard all the while they were in the classroom.

Twenty-nine years ago in 1961, when I was a high school sophomore, the Roseau Rams went to the State Hockey Tournament and beat all of the city teams to win the championship. History repeated itself a couple of days ago when Roseau became the 1990 state hockey champs. And I was there both times. I was surprised to find that the excitement was as great for me this year as it was when I was in high school. There was no denying the pride I felt watching those boys play hockey so masterfully they made the game look easy. It was clear from the beginning that our little high school of 364 students could hold its own among the city teams that have dominated the State Hockey Tournament for the last 13 years. It was equally clear after the first day of the Tournament that it wasn't going to be the city schools that would challenge Roseau but another northern town, Grand Rapids, only slightly bigger and equally committed. The championship game between the two top teams was one of the most singularly exciting sports events of my life. When Roseau won, 3-1, I was as proud of my hometown as I have ever been.

Bill Lund, the State's leading scorer and considered to be the best prospect to come out of Roseau since Neal Broten, was my favorite player. He looks, acts, and plays hockey very much like his father did, both at the high school and the college level. To the astonishment of hockey fans and professionals, Billy didn't score a single goal in the Tournament, a fact that resulted from a combination of bad luck—he hit the goal posts and the net—and a determination on his part to be a team player which made it possible for his wing man, Chris Gotziaman, to emerge a hero.

By the way, Zach, Tony, Willie and Chris almost got arrested for destroying the Foshay Tower, a Minneapolis landmark! Seriously, those boys drove us crazy while we tried to do a little shopping. They were even "lost" for a while, until a nice policeman returned them to us with strict orders not to let them out of our sight! The whole weekend was fabulous. We stayed at the old St. Paul Hotel, the same place I stayed for the 1961 State Hockey Tournament. Talk about *déjà vu!*

Dad and Wayne bought an Angus bull—1100 pounds, coal black, and $950. They took Jon and Roz with them to seal the deal. I stayed home to fix dinner, write, and revel in the solitude, with only my three dogs, two cats, the cows, Si (the bull), and the birds for company. My mood was melancholy. I kept thinking about our departure that is only two weeks away. I feel very sad about that. I know that I must go home; it would be dangerous to stay much longer. During the last few months I've become one with the farm. Except for missing Bill, I've been at total peace.

Roz and Jon came home with a huge brown hen egg in each hand and instructions from the farmer's wife to cook them for breakfast tomorrow. Rozie dropped one of hers and stared at the mess in disbelief. "Rozie," chided Jon, "you carried that egg all the way home from Williams and now you broke it!" She was devastated and wailed for quite a while. For once, she didn't have a comeback and let Jon get away with scolding her.

I snocatted over to Grandpa Clasen's today. I was feeling nostalgic about the fun we cousins used to have in the barn that Grandpa built. (It was the most impressive barn in the country.) We entertained ourselves for hours, swinging from a rope into new mounds of freshly-cut hay. The barn shows signs of decay now and, of course, the hayloft is empty. I can only imagine how many cows entered that barn, single file, to take their places at the stanchions, waiting to be milked. How many hay wagons came to fill the loft with sweet-smelling hay that provided the perfect landing for our swinging ropes? The memory of hay in a special barn so quickly transports me back to my childhood that it's hard to believe I'm not that child swinging from a rope anymore.

Spring has made an appearance in Northern Minnesota. The temperature has been in the 40s for the past few days and there is water everywhere. The boys and I bought Tingleys, tall water boots, so we can play outside and not worry about getting water in our boots. Roz and Jon splash in the puddles until they are forced to come inside because their clothes are soaking wet. It's a wonderful time of the year. Our anticipation of the 50 calves that will soon be born grows every day. Dad and

Wayne have been putting a couple of the most pregnant cows, those for whom birth is imminent, in the barn at night. Snow or freezing rain is forecasted for tonight, and we don't want a little calf to have to endure the harsh elements.

We watched Zach's last C Squirt hockey game the other night—actually, it was a scrimmage but the boys worked as hard as they did for all of their regular games. The game ended in a tie, with Zach making an assist. Zach has loved every minute of his hockey experience and agonizes over the end. But his thoughts are turning more and more to soccer these days as are Willie's. They've both started running with Katie and Linsay to get in shape.

Zach went to wrestling practice today and satisfied his curiosity about the sport. He said it was fun but didn't protest with his usual loudness when I said he couldn't join.

Tomorrow we're all going ice fishing. With the warm weather of the last few days, I hope the lake is still frozen enough! We have had good luck with fishing this winter, and the kids especially have had fun reeling in the walleyes.

The first little calf was born at 10:30 this morning. Wayne had put Lucille, his mother, in the barn last night and we were prepared to witness the event whenever it happened. But we missed it. When Dad went out to the barn to check on the progress, the feet were already sticking out, and by the time Roz, Jon and I got there, the little guy had been born. The mother licked him and was very rough at first. Wayne even thought that she may be trying to harm him. But his fears were allayed when she started nuzzling him. We visited the little calf periodically throughout the day. It took him almost two hours to find the mother's bag so he could suck. Just at the moment we thought we'd have to tie up the cow so the calf could be shown the bag, he started sucking. It was a huge relief because if calves don't get the colostrums within two hours of birth, they most likely will die. He is such a darling—little pink nose and four white-capped feet.

When the boys came home from school they rushed to the barn to admire the newest member of the bovine family who has, incidentally, been named Baby Jon. Later, when Mom came home, we all went out to pet him—no hugging yet though.

It's been raining all day. The path through the woods between Dad's and Wayne's is one long river, and the yard is spotted by little ponds. The barnyard is a mess. Rozie managed to get her boot stuck in the mud in her rush to see the new calf. Undeterred, she pulled it out but lost her balance in the process and fell down. Covered with mud and hoping to get some sympathy, she ran over to Jon who was wading in the pasture, but all he did was exclaim over and over about the wonders of waterproof boots, "Look, Rozie, my feet aren't wet at all!"

Fourteen

It's March 16th, and we're on our way to Joyce and Rod's for a supper of fresh walleye that we caught the other day. We woke up to a world of white again; it snowed all night and most of the day. It's been a fleeting encounter, this brush with spring. I was thinking yesterday how much I enjoyed the few days of warm weather. In another month, days like those will seem cool by comparison. For now though, the taste is enough. We have learned, here Up North, not to be greedy with spring.

My wanderlust must be strong these days, because I've been thinking about all of the places I'd still like to go—and the places I've been. I really do love to fly. Even today, having logged enough air miles to classify me as a veteran traveler, I still marvel at the experience. Unless I'm flying at night, I like to sit by the window and think about the blue hemisphere outside, altered only by the intense sunlight and occasional clouds. I find myself waxing pseudo-poetic—wondering if this flight, like the problem of sound, is really in existence with no one to observe or notice it. It's like being in a desert alone, utterly and completely—an island of life and silver in a sea of endless blue. Beautiful, perhaps, but it's ultimately indifferent, even hostile, to our existence. I still have that scary, helpless feeling when I stop to consider that I could be erased from the mind of man with no reaction from, or disturbance in, this surrounding beauty, in as little time as it takes a fully loaded plane to free fall

31,000 feet. Flying is—and always has been—for me a sobering and awesome experience.

Another calf was born between six and nine a.m. What a day to make her entrance into the world! Dad and Wayne are out in the pasture trying to get her and her mother into the barn. The calf's name is, of course, Baby Rozie.

The sky began to brighten in the late afternoon and finally the snow stopped. The gray has lifted and the world is brilliant in blue and white. It's so beautiful! The spruce trees and white pines wear the new snow like a sparkling gown.

The roads haven't been plowed yet, so the going is slow. A couple of times we've been closer to the ditch than my comfort level can stand! I'm happy about the temporary return of winter—I really am, because the beauty is breathtaking—but I know that there are many animals who are suffering or, at the very least, uncomfortable these days. For them, winter is a season to endure, a matter of survival. Not the least of those suffering is our new calf. Wayne brought her into Mom and Dad's house this morning, and she is now resting in front of the barrel stove. She's alive but still too weak to stand. So, even though my mouth is watering for walleye, I can't relax. We worked with our little calf all day—bottle feeding, holding her up to strengthen her legs, and messaging her chest to clear her lungs—and she looks better, but I'm worried that she'll take a turn for the worse while we're gone. If love and tender care can work miracles, she will recover because the boys have been hugging her every chance they get. She's so sweet and helpless.

It occurs to me that we all like to think of the wilderness, the country and its wildlife in neat, happy terms: the bull moose poised majestically on the road, timber wolves howling in the woods beyond the south forty; a beaver returning to its lodge at twilight, a freshly pruned branch between its teeth. Too many stories have been written where everything lives happily ever after. Children's books where the hunter kills the fawn don't sell. Nor, I suspect, would one in which the mama cow rejects her baby and the calf almost dies from neglect. But sometimes life in the country, in the woods, isn't pretty. The good guys don't always win. Nature can be cruel.

Today is Hannah Margaret Pearson's day. She will be baptized at the Roseau Evangelical Covenant Church this morning. Bill and I will be her sponsors (he in absentia). She looks adorable, dressed in white with pink trim and black patent leather shoes. In spite of full-blown winter, she smiles a lot. Nothing should spoil this day.

I have been up since 4:30 when Willie, Zach, Chris and I checked the pasture and found a new calf that had been born an hour or two earlier. We immediately woke up Dad who helped us get the cow and her calf inside the barn. The poor little thing was frozen stiff but we got him inside in time. We waited in the barn until 6:00 when we were sure that he had gotten the much-needed colostrums from his mother. When we checked at 8:00, mother and calf were doing fine.

Baby Rozie, the little calf we nursed back to health, turned out to be a feisty baby whose mother will nurse her only when we tie her up. She's kicked her calf so many times the little thing is tentative about approaching her. The other cows also kick her around whenever she gets near their calves. I feel so sorry for her. We give her supplemental bottle feedings, so she immediately starts rooting around when we enter the barn. She must think of us all as her substitute mothers!

Hannah's baptism was eventful in more ways than one. She calmly threw up all over while I was holding her in front of the church. Pam's sister, who was sitting in the front pew, handed me some Kleenex, which I used to clean Hannah off so she wouldn't soil the pastor's suit while he was presenting her to the congregation. When he took her, I was left with throw-up on the front of my jacket, exposed and clearly visible to all. Short of that little incident, it was a lovely ceremony.

After the party at Pam and Wayne's, where everyone enjoyed a delicious dinner, we were all sitting around the table when Wayne noticed five deer eating in the field west of his house. We watched them through binoculars, and I was once again filled with the wonder of the country where I always hope to experience wildlife in some form—the timber wolf howling from his den somewhere in the brush, the deer eating serenely in a nearby field, a mother fox playing with her kits south of the barn, a solitary moose poised in the middle of the trail, skunks carefully crossing the road in early spring. My world is so full of the predictable, I need a good dose of wonder once in awhile—happenings that make me just shake my head in awesome appreciation.

One of the most appealing things about living Up North is that the opportunities to discover the awe of life abound. We have some big country out our back door and four stimulating seasons in which to encounter it. I love to get out here—to feel the wind, taste the snow, find the magic that exists everywhere. I really learn to appreciate the fullness of things up here. There's a whole lot more going on then most people see.

Speaking of goings-on, this evening the North Country hosted one of its finest displays. The sun dripped over the horizon and sent shafts of pink up through the clouds. The sunset was so full of quiet I had to stop and listen to it. Not a branch bending, or a bird chattering, or snow crunching. Just quiet. I could hear my heart beat in my ears and my chest at the same time. I liked that. I thought about the way I left home almost four months ago—in a hurry, as usual, with last-minute details and discussions (in fact, I was planting tulip bulbs at midnight the night before I left!). Tonight will always have an asterisk beside it in my memories.

We had the 2:30 shift in the pasture and this time I had to make the rounds alone. I didn't want to interrupt the boys' sleep since they had school. All went well—no calves, thank goodness. The cows had frost all over them and their breath cut the night air like a giant scissors. Even though it was cold, the real sweet, real organic smell of spring permeated the air—so different from the clean smell of winter.

I don't know what made me think of the Northern Lights while I was roaming around the pasture. Maybe it was the star-studded sky, so bright that I hardly needed a flashlight. I used to know the scientific explanation of what makes the Northern Lights, but I've forgotten. I prefer to think of them as magic, anyway.

I remember one summer night's display in the North Country many years ago. I was on my way home from Warroad. It was late and I was tired. But I stopped the car to watch the magnificent show. And what a show it was! Great misty green shafts shot out of the northern horizon like a fireworks display you thought was over, but suddenly sent two or three more bursts of light into the night. Then, it wasn't just the northern horizon any more. It was all over and all the way to the top of the sky—if such a place exists. The lights swirled and snaked across a sky that was alive and shimmering with the green glow. I silently watched the awesome event for a long time. When I finally got into the car, the lights were still cavorting in the sky.

I'll admit that the few times since then that I've seen the Northern Lights (but never in such splendor as that night) I wonder all over again what makes them happen, but that's where I leave it. Some things are better with the wonder left in them.

Someone at church asked me why I came up here for four months. I was about to explain my objectives when I realized there was a simpler explanation that has to do with the importance of witnessing the Northern Lights. Being here in the North Country is good because it reminds me where the real world is and what it's made of—it's water and wind and wonder. Rarely do we have the opportunity to immerse ourselves in an experience that lets us look inside our souls, to explore our boundaries.

I had the opportunity to live Up North and I took it. When I lived here during my growing up days, I couldn't appreciate this country. All I could think about was leaving to explore new places and people. Now I've been given a second chance to fall in love. And I have—with the peace that comes over me when I'm watching the birds outside the front room window and feeling that all is right in the world, with the anticipation that bubbles inside when I think about all the potential the day ahead of me holds. "Up North" for me, from now on, will always be a time and place far from the here and now. It will always be a dream in the making, a tugging at my soul.

I know that sometimes when I'm staring deeply into the fire in my family room in Ohio, the images and sounds of the North Country will come back. It will feel so good. And I will know that I'm rich.

Today marks our last trip to Thief River. Because of the calving situation we couldn't leave until 11:00, so we got to Thief River just in time for dinner at Kentucky Fried Chicken. After grocery shopping at Hugo's we had coffee and a caramel roll at the Rex Café—our usual agenda. This is the first last of our stay here.

We've had three more calves—that makes a total of six born in the last week and a half. Baby Rozie, the little one we brought back to life beside the stove in the porch, is an orphan now. Her mother finally escaped from the barn, where we had her tied up in order for her calf to be able to suck, and now Baby Rozie is alone. Consequently, she thinks I'm her mother. I bottle feed her and give her the affection that I think every calf needs! The kids love to play tag with her, and they like it when she butts them around. I worry about her being in the dark barn by herself instead of romping outside with the rest of the calves. Dad says I could never be a farmer because I get too emotionally involved. I guess he's right. All of us have shifts at night when we go out to the barn and pasture to check the cows and calves. I'm pretty tired, having had only a few hours of sleep the past couple of nights. I love feeling needed though, and those little calves have won my heart.

On Monday night Zach and Tony played their Saturday morning league championship game. Malung won and the boys were happy! Zach's hockey career in Minnesota ended on an upbeat note. "I played well tonight, didn't I, Mom," Zach said as he was removing his skates, "I wonder when I'll wear these again." It's the second last of our sojourn in the Northland.

Last night we all went to the hockey game in Roseau. Gayle and Bill and the boys and Rozie were with us so the van was full and noisy. We were over half way home from the game when Gayle missed hearing Jon's voice and asked Bill to count heads. Sure enough, Jon wasn't in the car. I whipped the van around (reminiscent of the trip up here when we left Lucy on the toll road), and we broke the speed limit driving back to the Roseau arena. I heard Chris whisper, "What if he's been kidnapped?" This made Rozie wail, "Oh why didn't I take care of him!" I had barely stopped the van before everyone piled out and ran into the arena. There was Jon—sitting on the concession counter, munching on a hotdog. His first words were "Mommy, why did you leave me?" Roz, of course, had to pre-empt my explanation with her scolding, "Jon, you shouldn't have left us."

The story we got from Doug Hedlund who runs the concession stand (and later from Jonathan who freely talked about his experience) was that Jon approached a woman in the arena after the game and told her he was lost. She took him to Doug who asked him where he lived. He replied, "I live with my

Grandpa and Grandma on a farm in Minnesota—well, I really live with Uncle Wayne and Auntie Pam—but I'm from Ohio." Doug knew whom to call. He said that Jon was crying, but when he talked to Grandma who assured him that he was fine and we'd be back for him, he wasn't upset. He was so serious when he said, "I told Doug that you wouldn't want me to have candy, Mommy, so he gave me a hot dog."

Yesterday, Roz and Jon went to the library and then to Grandma's, as usual. Wouldn't you know it—Pam forgot to pick them up at Grandma's so they had to ride home with Bill an hour and a half later. Left again! That poor little guy is going to have a complex. His comment was, "Oh, that didn't matter, Mommy. We liked riding home with Uncle Bill. He bought us a treat."

Then Roz chimed in, "Jon, you weren't supposed to say anything because you know we're not allowed to have treats when it's suppertime. You're going to get Uncle Bill in trouble!"

I hope he won't be permanently damaged in any way because of these left behind incidents.

Tonight Willie and Zach went to their final Youth Group and Adventure Club meetings with Katie, Linsay, Jenny, Chris, and Tony. The kids in the Youth Group gave Willie a goodbye card signed by all of them. He was touched and asked me to keep the card in a safe place.

Our days are numbered—one week left to be exact. All of us are experiencing the mixed feelings of sadness to leave and excitement to get home. It's time. It's time to get on with our lives that have surely been enriched by this four-month sojourn in Minnesota. Bill is so happy that our homecoming is near. He says he's tired of having to explain to people why his wife took the kids and went home to her mother! I am eternally grateful to him for letting us have this experience. I can't help but hope that our marriage will be different now, that our separation will have healed all that has been so wrong. If that does, indeed, turn out to be the case, my sabbatical will have had an unexpected result.

No more calves. That's good because the weather is brutal.

Yesterday our seventh calf was born at 5 p.m. in the freezing cold. We got him inside the barn an hour later; he was disoriented form the cold but sucked eventually. He'll be okay. I hope that will also be the case with my little orphan who is lethargic today. I think it's because I fed her too much. She doesn't want to play tag with us; as a matter of fact, she doesn't want to move!

Last night I went out to the pasture at 2:30 a.m. to look for new calves—my usual shift. As I shone the flashlight over the frozen landscape I spotted an Angus who appeared to be nervous. Since her new calf was nearby, I respectfully stayed my distance. Cows can be dangerously protective if they think their calf is in trouble. Convinced that there were no new calves that needed attention, I started walking back to the barn. Out of the corner of my eye I could see the mother Angus pawing the ground and moving her head in a menacing way. I quickened my steps and then started running. I knew without turning around that she was running after me and I was scared stiff! I yelled but, of course, no one heard me. When I reached the fence, she was so close—I could feel her breath—I knew I wouldn't have time to crawl under it so I grabbed a stick and started brandishing it. She stopped, pawed the earth a few times, and retreated. I must have been yelling nonstop because I couldn't speak a word to Mom and Dad when I returned to the house. As it turned out, they had finally heard my screams and were on their way out the door to investigate. The incident, however, left me feeling no resentment or anger toward the cow. She was doing what all good mothers do—protecting her baby.

Mom took the day off to go gallivanting with Joyce and me. We went to Baudette to pick up carpet samples for her front room and then met Gayle for lunch in Warroad. We fooled around a little more before we decided to visit Helen Krueger who wasn't home, so we had coffee with her daughter and then with her son at his house. We arrived home just in time to feed Baby Rozie and help Dad and Wayne put some enormously pregnant cows in the barn.

It was fun spending the day with Mom whose company I've missed during our stay because of daily teaching. We just haven't had enough time together, so today was special. It would have been even more enjoyable if I could have talked! I think laryngitis has set in, and my ability to communicate in the time I have left will be sorely compromised.

I love to listen to repartee. It's a smart, competitive way of talking: one person makes a comment; another has a comeback; and a third has a retort. Bill and three of our friends can keep this up for several minutes without a pause. They enjoy each other and make this repartee look like easy communication. But it isn't easy. If it were, everyone who wanted to could do it. I would like to but can't. It will be good to hear it again.

At 6:30 we hurriedly packed some food and headed up to the hunting cabin—for the last time. Seven kids were with us. I feel guilty for abandoning the calving effort, but the prospect of uninterrupted sleep in the *Jakt Stuga* with all of the kids and my dogs fills me with warm anticipation

Fifteen

It's 8:30 in the morning. The hunting cabin has been alive with activity since 6:30. The kids and dogs have breakfasted and are now playing outside. Even though they are dressed warmly, the wind is so cold that they probably won't stay out for long. I worry about the pond that is twelve feet deep but probably not frozen solidly enough to hold up under pressure, so I'm sitting by the window to maintain careful vigil. The kids are playing "King of the Hill." Now that I think about it, I realize how silly it is to worry about a frozen pond in Minnesota that has endured four months of winter!

Even though I'm not a hunter, I can understand hunters and I think I know why a hunting cabin is important to their success. It's one thing to have a good hunt and go home. It is quite another to have a good hunt and go back to the cabin. Here you don't have to worry about tracking in dirt or deer hair. Nobody tells you what time supper will be ready and to get cleaned up. You don't have to watch your language or change your underwear. You can follow your instincts and satisfy your desires. You're on cabin time now—and there's always plenty of cabin time.

I've noticed that when hunters and non-hunters talk there is a gap, and I think it's because of the way hunters describe their experiences. Their talk is always of the way they dropped the big buck or just missed the one that got away. These are the success stories, the ones that are fun to tell—and fun to hear. To the listener, it must seem as if hunters are continually blasting away with shotguns and rifles when, in reality, they spend countless hours sitting on a deer stand listening to the November forest. I think hunters edit their entire experience in the woods. How else could the stories be so riveting!?

It has been a while, a long while, since I've been on the road. I can tell. I get itchy when I stop at a restaurant and see loaded snocats waiting for their riders to finish eating. I want to ride off with them. I feel a pang of envy when I see a hitchhiker, a serious longing when I hear a train whistle. I remember traveling in Europe one summer, when I hitchhiked during the day and slept on trains at night, not caring about destinations. A couple of weeks—maybe a month—of that would satisfy my wanderlust. There's still so much country to see.

In the days when my wanderlust was never allowed to get too strong, i.e., it was always satisfied, I was on the road a lot of the time. Some of my trips are memorable in their exotic challenges; others are memorable in their encounters with nature and people. All are memorable. I guess the one that presented the greatest physical challenge was my Nepal trip. When I think about that adventure, I not only remember the dangerous times but also that wonderful, free feeling of being on the move—seeing new country, putting a new perspective on the world, meeting the natural elements head on. I'm not sure what I was after when I decided to hike the off-beaten Tibetan path to the base camp at Mount Everest. Maybe I just wanted to see if I could do it. Or maybe I just wanted to have uninterrupted thoughts about a Peace Corps Volunteer I had fallen in love with in Thailand. For some reason, my last few days here have been preoccupied with this same desire: to enjoy uninterrupted thoughts about Bill—sweet thoughts filled with hope and anticipation. I'm excited to see him.

There's a passage from Steinbeck I like because it speaks about my wanderlust, which I probably will never "outgrow".

"When I was very young and the urge to be someplace else was on me, I was assured by mature people that maturity would cure this itch. When years described me as mature, the remedy prescribed was middle age. In middle age I was assured that greater age would calm my fever and now that I am 58 perhaps senility will do the job.

Nothing has worked. Four hoarse blasts of a ship's whistle still raise the hair on my neck and set my feet to tapping. The sound of a jet, an engine warming up, even the clopping of shod hooves on pavement brings on the ancient shudder, the dry mouth and vacant eye, the hot palms and churn of stomach high up under the rib cage . . . . I fear the disease is incurable." John Steinbeck, **Travels with Charley**

I'm back at the cabin by myself for a couple of hours of peace and solitude. We left here yesterday at 2:30 without completely cleaning up. After supper at Bolin's Café in Wannaska, Wayne and Pam, all of the older kids, and I went to a Christian rock concert at the Assembly of God Church. It turned out to be a stimulating evening—excellent music complete with stage effects, stirring message and testimonials, and an enthusiastic crowd. The kids were awestruck. They thought that Christian music, no matter what form, had to be boring. Were they in for a surprise! It was good to see young people so high on Jesus Christ instead of drugs—

This morning we went to church where Gayle, Pam and I failed abysmally at singing a special number. A combination of factors made it a weak performance: lack of preparation, my cow-induced laryngitis, a rocky start, and off-key alto. Gayle and I made a hasty exit, not wanting to put someone in the position of having to try and find something nice to say about our performance. Pam lingered and, I think, tried to explain our failure. The boys couldn't resist reminding us of all the sordid details on the way home.

145

Last week I gave a video presentation on my trip to Russia two years ago to the Covenant Women's Group in Roseau. My fears of sounding too liberal and pro-Russian for them were not realized. I received no feedback of that sort whatsoever. In fact, several women agreed that the USSR ought to try Socialism instead of Democracy, or the country will end up with homeless on their streets and old people in nursing homes (the two things Russians find most objectionable about the U.S.).

Willie and Zach helped Dad and Wayne castrate calves the other day. They decided this was a story to tell their friends back home! I was amused by their animated chatter that revolved around a variety of topics, including speculation as to whether the calves would ever be able to have babies. They kept expressing admiration for "Uncle Wayne and Grandpa who really know how to farm!"

I have two hours here at the *Jakt Stuga* before I go home and get ready for "Steel Magnolias," a play at the dinner theater in Warroad that we women are attending tonight.

The four months we've spent here in Northern Minnesota have been the best of everything, and now it is time for the boys and me to gather our belongings and head for home. It is a good time to leave. But what a magical interlude this has been! I shall miss a lot when I return home, beginning with this hunting cabin that has been my retreat away from what, I wonder. I do not know why, but this little space fills me with indescribable peace, even when it is rocking with kids' activity. I think I love the coffee, cooked the old-fashioned way, and the windows, allowing a full view of the outdoors, most of all. I hope this little cabin will always remain just the way it is now.

Now that I know my family so well I shall miss each even more than I did before my sabbatical. Mom is my mentor whom I happily see myself becoming more like every day. Dad is my anchor who started everything and keeps it going. I continue to see him as indestructible. I've grown to love my brother as the person hc is, not the person I thought he was based on my imaginings. I doubt that he can appreciate how grateful I am to him and Pam for letting us become a part of their lives for four months. My sister Joyce has risen to even greater heights of respect and admiration in my eyes. Gayle, the youngest of us three girls, has become a real person to me—sweet, competent, and complicated. My brothers-in-law are quite simply the best kind of people. And I like my sister-in-law even more now that I know her.

Probably the most revealing testament to the goodness of these people are their children—my nieces and nephews—whom I love very much. Each is special: sweet Katie who reminds me so much of myself at her age; Linsay who is unpredictable and endearing; Roslyn who has carved a forever place in my heart next to Jonathan's; Hannah who is perfect; Chris who is quietly growing up to be an intelligent young man, and his sister Jenny who is not-so-quietly growing up to be a beautiful woman; Tony who is, and I hope will always be, Tony; Sharon who is a wonderful mother, destined to be strong like her own mother; Shawn who is part girl, part woman, methodically carving out her own niche; and, last of all, Jena who will be the first female president of the United States someday.

One day I was driving down the empty road by my uncle's house and my parents' place at an unhurried pace, and I looked around as if I were seeing the countryside for the first time. It was early afternoon at the end of February, a winter day of bitter cold, frost, and bright cloudless skies. The sun shone, sending long shadows, but there was little warmth in it, and the plowed fields lay hard as iron. From the chimneys of scattered farmhouses smoke rose, straight as columns, up into the still air, and the cattle, incipient with pregnancy, gathered around fresh hay bales. I decided that I had never seen the familiar countryside look so beautiful, and I remember how sad I became when I realized that I shall miss it.

I have the same experience whenever I walk into my parents' house after I've been away. The familiar warmth and smells of the wood-burning stove greet me as I step into the porch, littered with boots and coats hung neatly on the rack or thrown on the chair. I meander about, opening cupboards, inspecting rooms, gazing from windows, touching furniture, straightening curtains—nothing is out of place; nothing has changed in the time I've been gone. If I'm tired when I arrive, I don't mind, because it quickly becomes a gentle tiredness, assuaged and comforted by my surroundings, as though the house were a kindly person, and I'm being embraced by loving arms. In the warm kitchen, sitting at the familiar table, I find myself filled with a sort of reasonless happiness. I am hit by the realization that time does not last forever, and I promise myself I will not waste a single moment. I love this house I grew up in. My spirits are renewed here. In this house, I hope that my mother and father will forever gather all the love and affection that their children have for them.

It's so important to have something to pass on, something by which we will be remembered. I want to leave behind things that talk of history, of friendship, of love—my journals and writing. I wonder if my children will someday want to know what I've written.

The trees of my farm are glistening in the sunshine, and my calves are romping in the pasture, but I'm in a panic. I'm babysitting the orphan calf (Baby Rozie) who is being treated to freedom and sunshine this morning. While making my pasture rounds, I discovered the bull was missing. He had broken out of his corral. When Dad didn't respond to my frantic cries for help, I began looking all over the farm for him. Having decided that he'd gone for a hike, I began searching for Si myself, because I knew he could do a lot of damage if he managed to get in the pasture with the pregnant cows. I finally found him frolicking in the pasture next to the cows but separated by a fence. He looked so free and happy to be near the cows once again. I didn't want to spoil that special pastoral scene, but I had to alert Dad who was returning from his hike. He said we had to wait until Wayne came home.

We now have a total of fourteen new calves, the newest having been born in the wee hours of this morning after I made the rounds at 3:30 and before Mom checked at 5:30. All are doing fine but not without effort on our part. One cow had a particularly difficult time and was in shock for about an hour afterwards, so she couldn't take care of her calf. We had to haul him into the barn in a wheelbarrow and get colostrums inside of him right away. Now his mother is very attentive.

Our little orphan is the most beautiful of the lot as a result of frequent bottle feedings. She runs up to us when we approach her and kicks up her heels, ready to play tag. The boys think she's wonderful. I wonder if she'll miss us when we're gone.

The highlight of these last couple of days was the observance of a birth from start to finish. Dad called me out to the pasture at 4:00 to observe the process and then hurried back to the house to get the boys who got off the bus at 4:20. It was an awesome experience for all of us. Zach exclaimed, "I never knew it would be like this!" Willie was grossed out at some stages, I think, but he too was impressed. He asked Dad, "Does it always go like this, Grandpa?" Calves are amazing animals. Ten minutes after they're born, they struggle to stand up and begin searching for nourishment. The cow licks her calf the entire time and urges it to follow her wherever she leads.

Wayne is the hero for the day. The boys love to relate (and embellish) the story of how he got the bull back in his corral single-handedly "with no weapon to protect him even!" It was a little disappointing in that all of us were charged up for a real battle, but Wayne's single-handed act of heroism was exciting enough.

Last night Gayle had a family surprise birthday party for me, one that I'll always remember. She had invited the boys and me for dinner but, because I had a bad cold, I was ready to call her and cancel. I was also babysitting Hannah who is cutting teeth, so she wasn't in the best mood either. However, when she told me that it would only be their family and mine, I decided to go. When I told Dad that Gayle was expecting the boys and me for dinner he said, "Oh, what time are we going?" I told him seven o'clock and he opened the door to announce the plan to Wayne who was just coming home. Well, to make a long story short, when I walked into Gayle's with Hannah in my arms and wearing my barn clothes, a chorus of voices (the entire family!) shouted, "Happy Birthday!" Despite my appearance and unhealthy demeanor, we had a wonderful time. I left carrying a huge poster filled with birthday wishes from my family.

It was another moment of pure joy in my family—laughs, lots of hugs, touching moments. It's why I always want to hurry back here, to the people who love me unconditionally. It's why I'm a Pollyanna. My family convinces me in so many ways that tomorrow will always rectify any bad things that happened today.

This is the second total surprise I've had in the time I've been here, the first being Bill's unexpected visit in January which Joyce and Rod masterminded.

Sometimes I look in the mirror, bewildered by the image facing me. "Who is this middle-age person?" Inside, I'm still young—searching for happiness, exploring possibilities, seeking to understand what I was put on earth to do. Is this everyone's secret—thinking that the better stuff has been left behind? Not mine. I think it's ahead.

A Note from Wayne to the Boys

Willie, Zach and Jon—I told Judy not to wake you so you could catch a couple more winks. I just want you guys to know it's been good to have you the last few months. I hope you all had a good time and memorable experiences. Take care now and we'll see you in July.

Love, Uncle Wayne

Sixteen

We've been back in Sylvania for a couple of weeks now. I'm watching Jonathan at his weekly gymnastics session. At the end of his first session after our return, he informed me that he had homework and asked if I'd like him to read one of the sheets of paper he had received (they were information sheets about the gymnastics program, etc.). Here's what he "read": "Children, listen to the music while you're skipping—Jonathan, please pay attention—now we're going to do some somersaults—Jonathan, are you listening?—now watch what I do—Jonathan, please sit down and listen . . . ." I asked him if his teacher had to tell him to behave many times and he replied, "Oh yes." The next session, after I had reminded him to listen to his teacher, this is what he reported: "My teacher says that I was better today than before and next week will be great." Pollyanna genes at work?

Jon will start swimming next week, much to his dismay. "I don't know why I have to take swimming lessons. Rozie doesn't," he lamented when I told him the news.

Willie and Zach are deeply involved in soccer and anticipating baseball. Their friends welcomed them back and, in some sense, it doesn't seem as if they've ever been gone—they just picked up where they left off. Every once in a while I hear them tell a story about Minnesota and engage in a "Remember when . . . ." or a "Wonder what . . . ." conversation. A couple of times I heard them express a desire to go back. For the most part, though, the joys of the present have already dimmed the memories of the past. I just hope that the years ahead won't erase them.

Not so with me. The memories are still so painfully real that I haven't been able to write. I miss everyone and everything. I yearn for those carefree, peaceful days when my biggest concern was what to make for dinner.

And yet, as much as my heart yearns for the country, I am, and always will be, essentially a suburban being. I spend a lot more time than I would prefer waiting at traffic lights, looking for parking places and sitting at a desk (writing my sabbatical report on teaching methods in a small, rural school). Mostly, I have to content myself with nightly walks with Lucy to reclaim my kinship with the natural world. Those walks are my chance to smell the air and watch the sky. Sometimes the rain falls in a fine spring mist, the kind I can't see until I look up toward the streetlight at the corner, and I think about snow falling gently to the earth. Not being interested in lofty human pursuits, Lucy uses the night walk to re-establish the boundaries of her territory—anointing streetlights, bushes, etc. I pause at the garage door so I can unsnap Lucy's rope from her collar. Inside I hang up my jacket. It had been a short rendezvous with the natural world—short, but for a suburban country girl, satisfying.

Tonight I'm remembering Northern Minnesota again— savoring the memory of the howling, swirling winds of winter and the damp, bone-chilling cold of the outdoors contrasting with the comforting warmth of the house we lived in for four months. I remember all the walks on the path between our two houses when my footsteps crunched in the snow, and the air was so cold it burned the inside of my nostrils. I remember looking up and watching a sky fill with snowflakes swirling to earth. I remember watching out the window in girlish wonder as wet, fluffy flakes clung instantly to everything they touched.

I remember being transfixed as shabby trees in the yard were transformed right before my eyes, as if the artist couldn't wait to finish the picture. I sip my coffee and savor the memory of the fairy tale scene. In my mind I see, taste, and smell another coffee—bubbling on the stove in a little hunting cabin tucked away in a small grove of trees.

So often, memories of the serenity of my Minnesota country experience fill me with a happiness that I wish I could bottle and then drink whenever I feel depressed.

> My Sister, My Friend—
>
> I shouldn't even try to write this—it's so hard to put my thoughts on paper—but I'm going to try. The last four months have been great. I have enjoyed just being able to run out and see you or pick up the phone and gab a little. We have gotten to know you again . . . We share so many of the same thoughts and feelings. I never thought you could ever enjoy being out on the farm—in the cow shit, mud and disorganization—how wrong I was. The love we share for Mom and Dad is so great. Our love for keeping memories alive and for the simple things in life are much the same. And the love we have for our kids . . . . Take a sabbatical on the farm every year. God bless you.
>
> Love, Joyce

Seventeen

Here I am, watching Willie play a great Pacesetter game. Moments ago he executed a smooth pass to his teammate who scored. I love being a Soccer Mom. It's a role that provides purpose as well as enjoyment. There aren't many things in life that afford me more pleasure than watching my sons run and dribble the ball on a soccer field. It's one of the rhythms of life. Right now, it's half-time so I'm resting alone under a tree on the side of the soccer field, keeping an eye on Jon who's picking dandelions with his girlfriends.

I let my thoughts wander as I write—this time to an old deer stand east of Gayle and Bill's that always came into view when snocatting last winter. It's hard to say how long that deer stand has been there. Its wooden framework has been weathered to the color of a November sky. Its platform boards—the ones still remaining—are warped and loose. Even the aspens that support the stand are dead and wobbly. One is half gone. Still, like a leaning tree that refuses to fall, the stand hangs on. It sits there, soaking up the winter sunshine.

I wonder if any hunter will ever again sit upon the stand. I don't think it has any value as a hunting stand anymore, but it will be there, just the same. It will sway when the wind moves the trees, just as it always has. Maybe someone will fix it up so it can be used this year.

I don't know who built that stand—probably my father or my brother or maybe a neighbor. It's very simple. It consists of a couple of two-by-fours nailed between two trees, with a few flat pieces across the top for a platform. It's about 18 inches wide at its broadest point and perhaps six feet off the ground. That's all there is.

I can't help but wonder what memories this simple stand has to share. How many frosty mornings did someone sit there and shiver in the cold? How many empty cartridge casings were ejected into the grass below? How many candy bars were eaten? How many cigarettes were smoked? How many mornings did a hunter watch the sun rise from the cluster of pines to the east? How many of those days did he watch the sun disappear over the western horizon?

How many times did the stand feel a hunter's heart beat as he watched a buck work its way out of the woods, pause, and flick his big ears back and forth? How many times did the hunter's bullet find its mark? How many times did it pass harmlessly in the trees beyond?

And what of the hunter who once used this spot? Is he like the boards themselves—maybe my Dad—older now, weathering gracefully with the years? Or maybe he was a neighbor who's gone the way of the aspens, his stand a memorial to some of his most pleasant hours on Earth.

Perhaps during this deer season, a buck or a doe will meander through the trees, nibbling twigs as it goes. It will stop in the clearing, head up, ears perked. It will wait. But no shot will ring out from the stand.

We're on our way to Zach's soccer game in Lima, Ohio. Willie went to the OM (Odyssey of the Mind) competition in Columbus with his friend, so it's just the four of us and one of Zach's Pacesetter soccer friends who's riding with us. Zach is telling Ted stories about his Minnesota experience—watching

"Dennis the Menace" at 4:30 when they got home from school, ice fishing, snocatting, life on the farm (even the birth of a calf—in detail). I like that.

Judy—

It's about 10:30 at night and I'm canning tomato sauce! I've been wanting to drop you a line so I figured this was the best time. All of the children are in bed and Wayne is working, so I have some peace and quiet.

I just wanted to let you know how much I miss having you around. It was so nice this winter not to have to rush off to work all of the time . . . .

I'm so glad that the boys could drop in whenever they felt like it (especially Jonny!). I hope all three of them will remember our house and always feel comfortable here. Of all the things the boys did, I'll miss Jon's entrances and exits most of all. The bigger boys were so busy with other things, but Jon was counting on me being home whenever he decided to drop by. He's quite a kid! I'll never forget this winter!

. . . . Katie's best friend moved, so she has some adjusting to do. Linsay is having a good time at school, having met and befriended a little girl. As she gets friends, I'll feel less worried about her. Oh, of course, Roz misses Jon; she has no one to boss around now. And Hannah keeps growing . . . .

Love, Pam

Eighteen

Several weeks have passed since my return. My life has assumed a kind of routine normalcy that was expected, and I'm glad to be in my own home again with my husband and children. Until just recently, though, I missed everyone and everything in Minnesota so deeply that I couldn't linger on a memory without a lump rising in my throat.

As far as Bill is concerned, I think that separation has done its job; at least it has made me appreciate him more. I'm trying to get rid of the notion that I want Bill to be a certain way, that it is my job to make him different. Who knows? Our relationship might have never-before-seen new possibilities. Maybe he'll want to go on walks with me now—but if he doesn't, I'll try not to take his response as personal rejection.

Writing about my marriage at a time when I felt it was out of my control has helped me to understand it better, I think.

Lucy is only now emerging from a period of mourning her lack of companionship with Toby and Charlie. Those three dogs became my constant companions on the farm—like Jon and Rozie. Sleek and beautiful Toby always beat the ground with her tail in her happiness to see me. She never overcame her resentment of Lucy, when the latter was allowed in the house while she was barred from the premises.

What a contrast scruffy Charlie made! He was no less eager to greet me but, instead of outwardly expressing his enthusiasm, he would wait patiently until I gave him attention. His sad eyes—in fact, his entire doleful expression—won a lasting place in my heart.

Some of my happiest moments were spent driving to Roseau to pick up the kids with all three dogs settled comfortably in the van. They did not like to be left behind. I even left the van door open to provide sanctuary for Toby and Charlie on cold, blustery days when no one was home at their respective houses, and they weren't allowed inside. I wonder if they've forgotten the van. Have they forgotten me?

The beauty of the farm itself is still heart-wrenching. I'm glad I savored the sunsets (and more than a few sunrises), because they are forever etched in my mind, and I can recall them by closing my eyes. I can also readily conjure up the blackness of the nights when there was only heavenly light. I've said it before: There is no sky like a Northern Minnesota sky.

If the skies comforted me at night, the landscape calmed me during the day. I don't think I will ever again feel the peace and tranquility that marked my existence on the farm. Standing on Wayne and Pam's deck afforded me a view of their land and made me feel at one with it. The excitement of discovering a herd of deer feeding in the field was secondary to the knowledge that they were there every morning, and I was only rediscovering their presence. The howl of the timber wolf filled me with unspeakable joy. I wanted to shout to affirm Nature, to celebrate the wolves' superiority over man.

The cattle were another symbol of tranquility. My last week home, I couldn't get enough of the peaceful pastoral scene. When the little calves were born and their mothers nurtured them, I was convinced that all was right with the world. I even enjoyed the responsibility of my nightly pasture checks. So many times I still think about the little orphan calf and wish I could bury my face in her soft hide.

There's a lot more I could say, most of which probably doesn't need to be said, after all. I will treasure forever the carefree days I spent with my father, brother, nieces and nephews, and my boys. I will treasure forever the stolen moments with my mother. And I will treasure forever the giving relationships I formed with my sisters, sister-in-law, and brothers-in-law.

I'm always surprised to be reminded of how wild Northern Minnesota is. It is said that one can walk the North Woods for days and never see man. Our state possesses more predators, including the timber wolf, than any other state in the lower 48. I believe that no other state can be so wild, so diverse, so beautiful through the change of seasons. The lure of escape from the tensions of the city can be experienced year after year.

But it takes special people to live up there—people who choose to be there through the severest of winter. My family is made up of special people. I just hope they don't forget what they have—don't take the serenity of country living for granted. Screaming sirens, the threat of crime, long lines of traffic, the harshness of the city—these things simply don't exist up there. I hope that it will always be so.

May 17, 1990

Dear Judy,

I'm going to do something a little useful with my break and write you a note. I'm on the night shift and I usually go out for some fresh air but it's really cold and windy.

Dad and I have been in the field again. It sometimes gets too busy and hectic but most of the time I really enjoy being out there. I guess I just enjoy farming. We need rain though. It's too dry for everything—pastures, hay and crops. It's going to come soon, I hope.

We had our last calf on May 3rd. It was that old red and white cow that had such a big belly—Tubby was her name at the end. Calving went so good this year—we never lost a single one. I really appreciated your help with all those night shifts. You just about got done in because of it though.

It was lonely and sort of empty around here for a while after you guys left. Coming home from work and having coffee and your baked goodies was always something to look forward to. It was fun getting to know my oldest sister. You know, you and I are a lot alike. I noticed so much how you got pleasure and satisfaction out of doing just simple things.

I hope I can show my girls that taking a ride up on the ridge or going for a picnic is just as satisfying as going shopping or ordering a pizza. It's so easy to get caught up in all the hustle and bustle of life, and a lot of times it's the simple things we do together that we'll remember most.

I enjoyed having the boys around, seeing how their minds worked and getting to know them a little bit. It was fun watching them as they saw new experiences, the questions they asked and the interest they showed. I hope they can come and stay with us for summer vacations.

Rozie talks about Jon so much. She really misses him. Every once in a while she asks me what I think Jon is doing . . . . Take care of yourself.

Love, Wayne

Nineteen

In a letter from Gayle this fall, she described how Tony made a promise to his parents that he was going to change his ways in school and not get into so much trouble. He allowed as to how this promise might be a little easier to keep now that he was older and Zach was gone. Gayle said that the first day of his new life was "awesome". He prayed for about 20 minutes the night before school started. She heard him telling the Lord how he was really going to change this year. On and on—well, that lasted for about a week. The next Monday he came home and informed her he was tired of trying to be so good and that he thought he would just go back to the way he was. Then, the following day Gayle got a call from the bus driver telling her that Tony would soon have to walk to school if he did not shape up. I can just hear her lament: "Where, oh where, did I fail?!"

She went on to say that Chris was deep into the hunting scene. Apparently, she had to pick up licenses for him—bow license, deer license, and partridge license—all to the tune of $75. When she confronted him with the expense, he looked at her "with that face he gets" and said, "But, Mom, I am going to provide meat for the family for the whole winter." I can just hear Jenny scoffing at that claim!

It won't be long before the coffee pot will be working overtime at the *Jakt Stuga!*

While my sabbatical didn't fit the academic mold in that most of the work I did was not scholarly, I don't think the University will consider it a waste of time and money. Given the fact that I was eager to return to the classroom this fall, I would have to say that I am at least refreshed and have a renewed dedication to teaching. I submitted my sabbatical report, which included a case study of teaching children how to read in a small, rural Minnesota school. I necessarily left out the details of my experience that will burn in my memory forever. For example, there was no mention of cornbread, Northern Lights, or wolves.

Mom and Dad's 80th birthday party at Bemis Hill

Some Minnesota Moments

Getting ready for a snocatting expedition

Zach at the height of his hockey career

Some Minnesota Moments

Who's having fun here?

Can't get wet with our Tingleys on!

Some Minnesota Moments

Mom enjoying a conversation with her students

Jon and Roz at Malung School
(note the "Good Student" tags!)

Some Minnesota Moments

Enjoying a moment with the newest member
of the bovine family

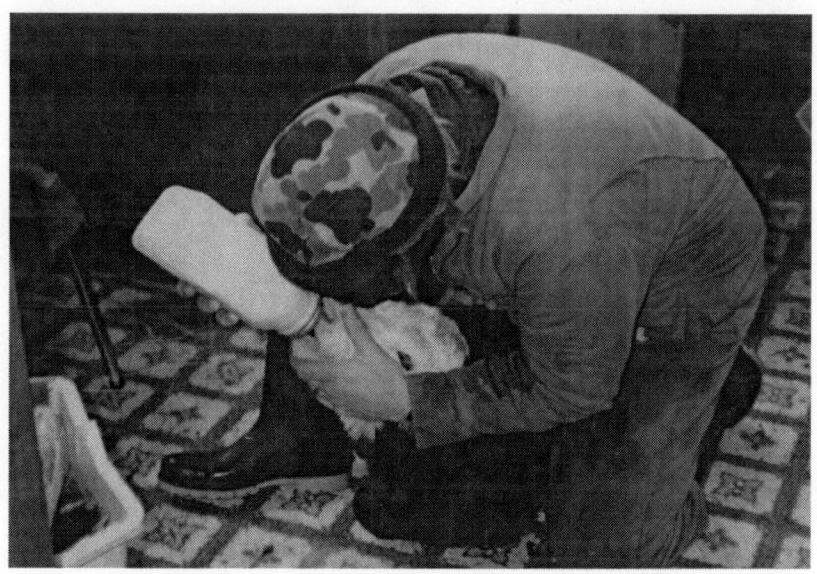

Nursing the orphan calf back to health

Some Minnesota Moments

Will's farewell at Youth Group with Pastor Joe

Kings of the Hill at the hunting shack